The University of Virginia

A Pictorial History

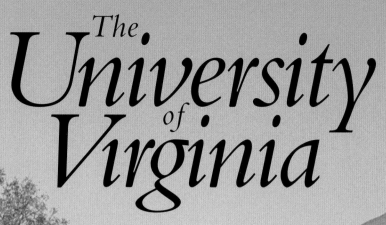

The
University
of
Virginia

A PICTORIAL HISTORY

Susan Tyler Hitchcock

UNIVERSITY PRESS OF VIRGINIA

and

UNIVERSITY OF VIRGINIA BOOKSTORE

Charlottesville and London

The University Press of Virginia and the University of Virginia Bookstore
© 1999 by the Rector and Visitors of the University of Virginia
All rights reserved
Printed in Hong Kong

Designed by Gibson Design Associates

First published 1999

The paper used in this publication meets the minimum requirements of the
American Standard for Information Sciences—Permanence of Paper for Printed
Library Materials, ANXI Z39.48-1984.

Library of Congress Cataloging-in-Publication Data
Hitchcock, Susan Tyler.
    The University of Virginia : a pictorial history / Susan Tyler
Hitchcock.
        p. cm.
    Includes bibliographical references and index.
    ISBN 0-8139-1902-9 (cl. : alk. paper)
    1. University of Virginia—History. 2. University of Virginia—
Pictorial works.   I. Title.
LD5678.H58 1999
378.755'481—dc21

                                                99-18167
                                                CIP

Contents

Acknowledgments

I wish to extend special thanks to Garth Anderson, Jason Bell, Raymond Bice, Cindy Garver, Erin Garvey, Allan Gianniny, Tiffany Gilbert, Sandy Gilliam, Lucien Howard, Margaret Hrabe, Robert Kellogg, Phyllis Leffler, Heather Moore, Mary Murray, Pauline Page, Jeanne Pardee, Michael Plunkett, Ed Roseberry, Regina Rush, Bill Sublette, Jack Syer, Kim Vierbuchen, and Mic Wilson. I especially wish to express my gratitude in memoriam to Joseph L. Vaughan and to thank those people, listed as sources, who offered their time during personal interviews and subsequent conversations.

This project could not have been accomplished without the working partnership of the University Press of Virginia and the University of Virginia Bookstore. In this time when scholarly presses and university bookstores face new challenges in the marketplace, this book stands as an example of synergy beneficial not only to the publishers but to the friends and alumni of the university that they represent.

There is no way that the short text of a book like this one can adequately recognize by name every individual who has contributed to the colorful and distinguished history and current reputation of the University of Virginia. To those who have given of their energy and intelligence but who go unnamed on these pages, thank you.

Foreword

The history of the University of Virginia is unique. Unlike the great schools of Europe, this university did not evolve slowly from religious houses, did not spring to life through royal charter or develop to serve the needs of a metropolitan or industrial center. It differs also from the well-known educational institutions of this country: the University is not a land grant college, or a private school founded by a great philanthropist, or a modern descendant of a colonial college for preachers or teachers. Instead, this place is the direct result of one man's practical vision of education for the free citizens of a new democratic nation.

Even more clearly than his brilliant contemporaries, Thomas Jefferson saw the necessity to educate citizens, and he conceived that mission broadly. He believed that participatory government requires that the participants be educated, both in the "useful sciences" of the day and in the history of other systems of governance. To be wise practitioners of their rights, citizens of the new republic needed to be versed in their duties. To guard the young democracy against future "degeneracy" and the "indigence of the greater number," Jefferson wanted to create a means to cultivate natural leaders ("persons, whom nature hath endowed with genius and virtue") to be groomed as protectors of the rights of all. He intended his University to be the nurturer of these persons.

When we walk across the Grounds today, we may not appreciate how radical these ideas were in their time. We may not see ourselves as parts of the ongoing experiment of a genius. Perhaps we take comfort from the apparent age of the place and the beauty and variety of its architecture. Quite often we may fall back into an idea of tradition. For example, we may take for granted the notion of the university as a meritocracy, or assume the appropriateness of state support. We may find uncontroversial

the idea that, on the whole, a public school's mission is secular. We may be unamazed that undergraduates are allowed to choose their own courses of study.

Two hundred years ago these were not commonplace assumptions. They became so because of experiences here. The Jeffersonian design manifest in our bricks and values and practices now seems traditional only because it has proved itself over time and been adopted by most of American higher education. To forget its origin is to misunderstand this young and remarkably vital Academical Village.

The book you hold, astutely written by Susan Tyler Hitchcock and handsomely published through a unique partnership between our own University Bookstore and University Press, will help to explain and strengthen Thomas Jefferson's legacy as the creator of a great institution built on principles of free inquiry, honor, and public service. The physical University is well represented. Many of these photographs are published here for the first time, thanks to the generosity of Special Collections at Alderman Library, the Alumni Association, and many individual friends and alumni. To all involved with the production of this fine history, and to all its readers who care so deeply about the University that they choose to understand both its physical beauty and the irrepressible spirit that formed it, I am grateful.

JOHN T. CASTEEN III
President of the University of Virginia

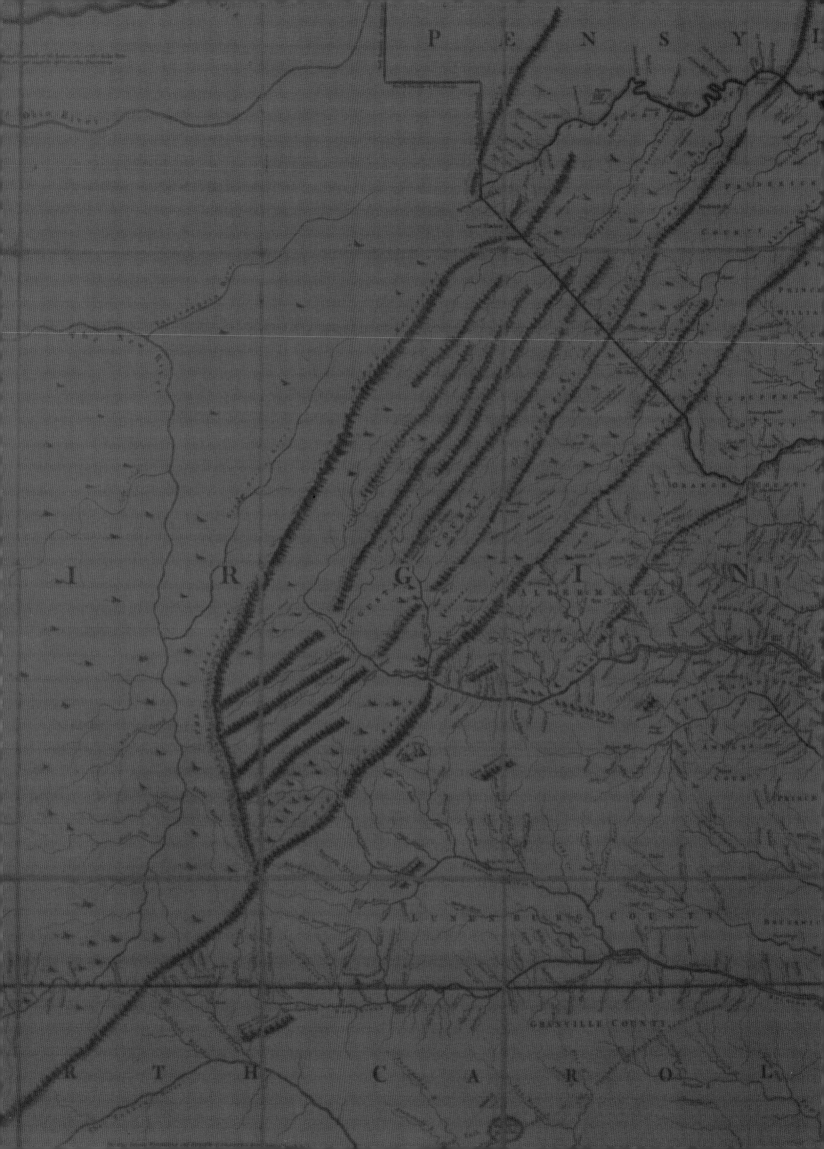

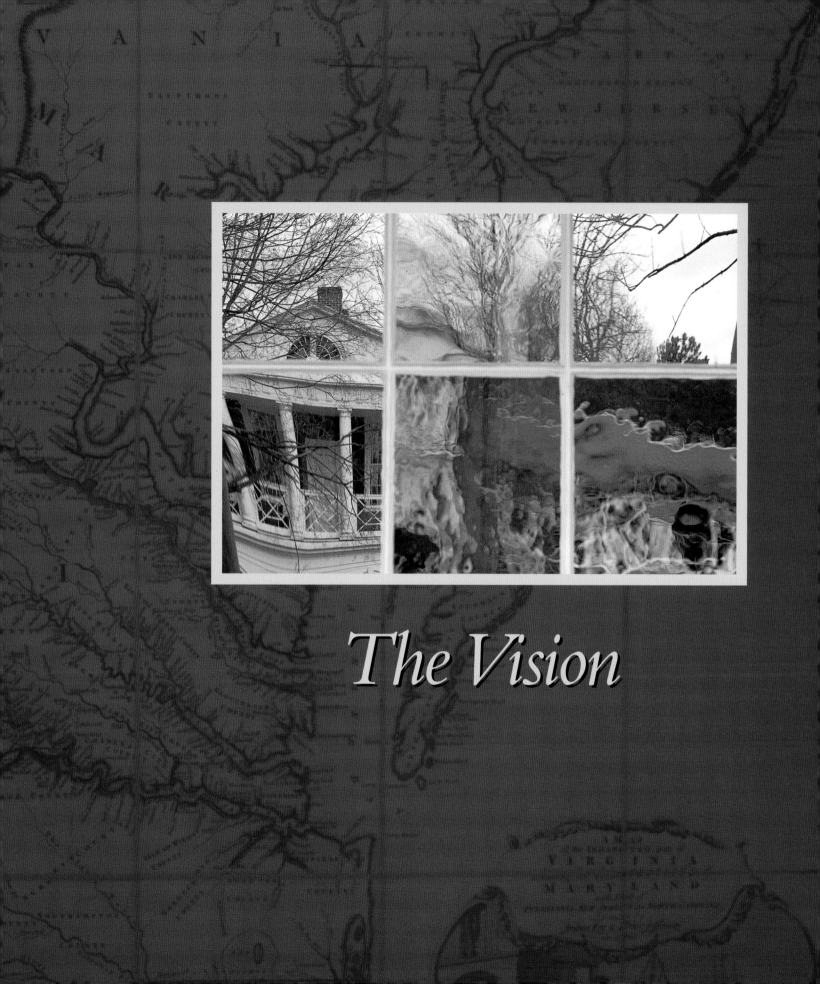

The Vision

Thomas Jefferson

In 1744, the year after Thomas Jefferson was born, the General Assembly of Virginia created Albemarle County. The terrain must have been, to use Jefferson's own language in *Notes on the State of Virginia,* "placid and delightful," "wild and tremendous." A year later, Albemarle property holders met in Scottsville and commissioned themselves as county magistrates. Among them was Peter Jefferson, father of Thomas, one of the county's first settlers, who had moved from Richmond in the 1730s and received a patent for one thousand acres, later increased by several hundred more.

In 1761, when Thomas Jefferson was eighteen and attending the College of William and Mary, county fathers moved the seat of government to the county's center, turning a plot of fifty acres into the grid of a town and naming it Charlottesville, after George III's queen. Between 1790 and 1820 the population of Albemarle County grew to twenty thousand, including ten thousand slaves. In 1818 Charlottesville comprised eighty-two household lots and a new two-acre public square. To the west of town stretched fields and forests.

1818

Education ... engrafts a new man on the native stock, and improves what in his nature was vicious and perverse into qualities of virtue and social worth.

— *Thomas Jefferson, 1818*

Peter Jefferson's map of Virginia.
When Peter, Thomas Jefferson's father, and Joshua Fry, Albemarle County's first surveyor, printed this map of Virginia in 1751, Charlottesville was at the western edge of European-settled territories.

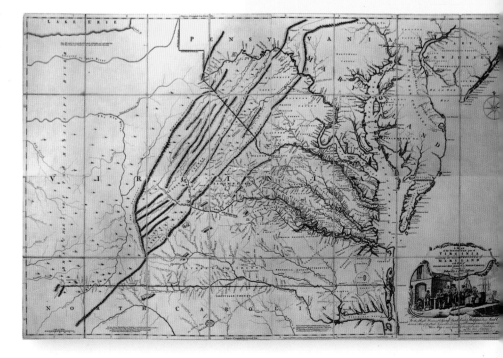

Virginians of means hired teachers for their children or sent them to private academies, often run by clergymen, as was the academy run by Reverend James Maury in Shadwell that Thomas Jefferson attended. Young gentlemen with aspirations attended the College of William and Mary, or perhaps Princeton or Harvard. Professional studies proceeded through apprenticeships, typified by Jefferson's five years in George Wythe's law office in Williamsburg.

In the decades after the Revolution, American education changed rapidly. Between 1782 and 1802, nineteen new colleges were founded, including state-chartered institutions in North Carolina, Tennessee, Vermont, and Georgia, although none comprehensive enough to be considered a university. Jefferson, by that point Virginia's governor, proposed to develop the College of William and Mary—which had been chartered in 1693 by the crown and the Church of England—into a more diverse institution and make it the ward of the commonwealth. The college's Board of Visitors did not agree to all his proposals, but they did abolish professorships of divinity and add faculty in law, medicine, and modern languages.

The College of William and Mary. *In Thomas Jefferson's youth, the only college in Virginia was William and Mary, chartered in 1693.*

Although some presumed that William and Mary would remain the state's center of higher education, Jefferson turned his sights elsewhere. In 1820, when his grandson Francis Eppes came of age, Jefferson sent him instead to South Carolina College; and he discouraged a friend's son from teaching at William and Mary, which was suffering such a decline in students, faculty, and vision that Jefferson called it an educational cul de sac. The buildings in Williamsburg were, according to a visitor of the time, "tending rapidly to ruin." Instead of renovating the old, Jefferson, who had kept a home at the nearby Monticello since 1809, began to envision a new state university in Charlottesville.

Jefferson's Ideals of Education

Education was essential to the new republic in Thomas Jefferson's view—an education available universally, not just to those who could afford it. In 1779, even before becoming governor of Virginia, he had introduced to the General Assembly his "Bill for the More General Diffusion of Knowledge," arguing that education should prepare those with "genius and virtue" for the task of protecting the rights of all citizens and guarding the democracy against "degeneracy." The bill was not passed, but its passionate language reveals how central an ideal education was for Jefferson. "It becomes expedient for promoting the publick happiness," the bill read, "that those persons, whom nature hath endowed with genius and virtue, should be rendered by liberal education worthy to receive, and able to guard the sacred deposit of the rights and liberties of their fellow citizens, and ... they should be called to that charge without regard to wealth, birth or other accidental condition or circumstance."

To ensure that "the indigence of the greater number" did not impede the selection and training of the best leaders, Jefferson proposed that state districts provide primary schooling for all "free children, male and female," and secondary schooling for those who excelled (chosen "from among the boys" only), and "by this means twenty of the best geniusses will be raked

We wish to establish in the upper country, and more centrally for the State, an University on a plan so broad and liberal and modern, as to be worth patronizing with the public support, and be a temptation to the youth of other States to come and drink of the cup of knowledge and fraternize with us.

— *Thomas Jefferson, to Dr. Joseph Priestley, 1800*

Monticello. *Jefferson resided at Monticello, only a few miles from Charlottesville, until his death in 1826.*

from the rubbish annually." Of those, each district would select one student "of the best learning and most hopeful genius and disposition" to support at the highest level of education.

Jefferson's early stands on education foreshadow key features of his university: a state-supported, nonsectarian school, available to many and dedicated to advancing knowledge in modern and classical fields of study. These elements form our contemporary notion of a state university, but in Jefferson's time the idea was revolutionary.

Albemarle Academy and Central College

Albemarle County had in 1803 been granted state permission to establish an academy, or secondary school, but not until 1814 did county leaders plan the school in earnest. Jefferson seized on the provision, seeing in it potential for a university. "I mentioned to you that it had long been in contemplation to get a university established in this State," he wrote to a friend. "We are about to make an effort for the introduction of this institution." When Peter Carr, Jefferson's nephew and president of the academy board, forwarded Albemarle's proposal to the General Assembly, the school's name had been changed to Central College.

The six members of Central College's Board of Visitors—Thomas Jefferson, James Madison, James Monroe, state senator Joseph C. Cabell, General John H. Cocke, and state delegate David C. Watson—were to meet in April 1817. Only Jefferson, Cabell, and Cocke attended; but they proceeded with plans, inspecting property earlier owned by Monroe. Jefferson's overseer, Edmund Bacon, described the college site as an "old, turned-out field," but the visitors found the two hundred acres "high, dry, open, fur-

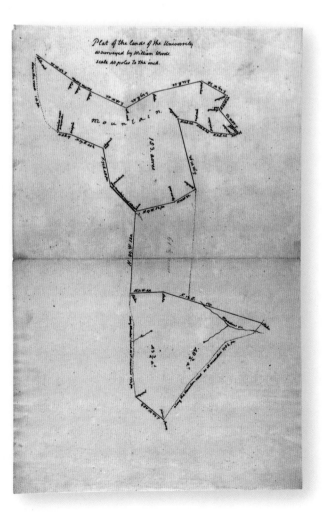

Lands of the Central College. *In 1817 Jefferson and fellow advocates of higher education in Virginia (including James Madison and James Monroe) secured the state's permission and funding to purchase property earlier owned by Monroe on which to build Central College. Five months later the General Assembly agreed the property should support not a college but the University of Virginia.*

nished with good water, [and with] nothing which could threaten the health of students." By September 1817 the land had been purchased with state money for the price of $1,518.75, raised by the sale of escheats (land left without an heir) and deserted glebes (church property). Further financial support came through private subscriptions, including $1,000 from Jefferson. By the end of 1817, the board had $35,102 in hand and another $8,000 in pledges. On 6 October 1817, President James Monroe laid the cornerstone for Central College, at the site of what was to become Pavilion VII.

James Monroe, fifth United States president.
A neighbor to Thomas Jefferson, Monroe was interested in the University of Virginia from its earliest conception. He was on the Central College Board of Visitors, which secured the land for the academical village, and while president he attended the ceremonial laying of the cornerstone for the first university building, Pavilion VII (left), on 6 October 1817.

Reporting on Central College to the House of Delegates in January 1818, Jefferson used words and images that bring to mind the university's Lawn today. "Instead of constructing a single and large edifice," he and the other college visitors "thought it better to erect a small and separate building, or pavilion, for each professor they should be able to employ, with an apartment for his lectures, and others for his own accommodation, connecting these pavilions by a range of dormitories, capable each of lodging two students only, a provision equally friendly to study as to morals and order." He dared to suppose that the legislature might "think proper to proceed to the establishment of an University" on the site of Central College.

The Meeting at Rockfish Gap

Joseph Cabell was Thomas Jefferson's legislative liaison, and it was through him Jefferson hoped to hear that the Senate and House of Delegates had agreed to fund a university in Charlottesville. It was a difficult political battle, with Cabell pitted against those who preferred to build an elementary school system first, those who favored a centralized state system for providing education to the poor, and those who considered regions west of the Blue Ridge the true center of Virginia.

Early designs for the academical village. *Jefferson corresponded with William Thornton and Benjamin Henry Latrobe, exchanging drawings and ideas of how the university's central buildings should be arranged. Early drawings projected larger buildings joined by a string of smaller rooms. The concept of a prominent Rotunda did not evolve until later in the planning process.*

Central College board minutes, 1819. *Meeting for the last time as visitors of Central College, officials (including Thomas Jefferson and James Madison) agreed to turn all funds from the college over to the University of Virginia, now authorized by the Virginia legislature. The minutes of their last meeting, dated 26 February, indicate their intention to apply all funds "to the providing additional buildings for the accomodation of the Professors, & for dieting & lodging the students."*

12

approve of the propositions for covering with tin sheets the pavi-
-lions and hotels hereafter to be covered, and for bringing water
to them by wooden pipes from the neighboring highlands.

That Alexander Garrett, treasurer of the Central college,
be continued as the depository of the funds of the institutions,
with authority to exercise the powers and perform the duties of
Bursar of the University until otherwise provided.

That to meet the immediate and pressing calls for money
he be authorised to recieve from the treasury of the state the sum
of fifteen hundred Dollars, in part of the public endowment of 15,000.
Dollars for the present year.

That a copy of these proceedings be laid before the Governor and council for the exercise of the power of controul committed to them by the same act of the legislature, should they think
proper to exercise that power on any part of these proceedings

18

Feb. 26. 1819.

Th: Jefferson

James Madison

J. H. Cocke

David Watson

We the subscribers, Visitors of the Central College, having been
specially called to meet on the 26th day of Feb. 1819, and au-
-thorised by the act of the legislature, now in session, for establish-
-ing the University of Virginia, to continue the exercise of our
former functions, and to fulfill the duties of our successors, Visitors
of the sd University, until their first actual meeting, have una-
-nimously agreed in the following opinions & proceedings.

That it is expedient that all the funds of the University,
applicable to the services of the present year, which shall remain
after meeting all the other current & necessary purposes, shall
be applied to the providing additional buildings for the
accomodation of the Professors, & for dieting & lodging the
students of the University.

That the urgency of the advancing season, & the importance
of procuring workmen before they become generally otherwise
engaged for the season, render it necessary for expediting the
objects of the University, that certain measures be forthwith
taken, which, if delayed until the first actual meeting of our
successors, would materially retard those objects.

That taking into view the balance remaining of the
funds of the last year, to wit, of the proceeds of the glebes, &
of the 1st & 2d instalments of subscriptions, after payment
shall have been made of the expenditures of the same year,
as also the 3d instalment of subscriptions payable in April 1820
and the public endowment of 15,000. D for the present year,
engagements may be entered into for building in the
approaching season two more pavilions for the Professors,
one Hotel for dieting the students, and as many additional
Dormitories for their lodging, with the necessary appendages
as the said funds shall be competent to accomplish: that we

In February 1818, Jefferson and Cabell enjoyed a partial victory. The General Assembly appropriated fifteen thousand dollars to found what they named the University of Virginia, "wherein all the branches of useful science shall be taught," its location yet to be determined. A board of commissioners, one from each senatorial district, was to meet on 1 August at the tavern at Rockfish Gap, midway between Charlottesville to the east and Staunton and Lexington to the west, the three sites contending for the university. The commission was to recommend location, building plan, academic agenda, and professorial needs.

Jefferson was chosen unanimously as president of the commission. Discussion began by comparing the three towns. Which would provide the most healthful environment? Which offered the most fertile terrain nearby? Which included the greatest assets? Which was the closest to the center of Virginia? Washington College (later Washington and Lee) in Lexington could promise a three-thousand-acre estate and a private subscription of $17,878; however, Central College, on two hundred acres, had private subscriptions of $41,248 and a pavilion and twenty student rooms already constructed. Jefferson argued further, dividing the map by population (considering white males only) and geography, that Charlottesville lay closest to the center of the state.

The commissioners voted sixteen to five in favor of Charlottesville as the location for the University of Virginia. Conversation proceeded to the matters of design and instruction. In its report to the General Assembly, written in the main by Jefferson, the commission recommended a lawn lined by pavilions, each containing lecture rooms and faculty apartments. Adjoining each pavilion would be a string of dormitory rooms, with occasional hotels for dining, a weather-worthy passage connecting them all. The commission considered this design "advantageous to morals, to order, and to uninterrupted study" and proposed a larger building in the middle.

The pavilions. *From early on—as shown in this 1814 elevation and plan—Jefferson envisioned two-story pavilions for faculty, which were attached to single-story student dormitory rooms.*

Areas of study proposed by the commission numbered ten, each to be headed by a single professor.

1. *Ancient languages (Latin, Greek, Hebrew)*
2. *Modern languages (French, Spanish, Italian, German, Anglo-Saxon)*
3. *Pure mathematics (algebra, geometry, military and naval archi-tecture)*
4. *Physico-mathematics (mechanics, statics, dynamics, pneumatics, acoustics, optics, astronomy, geography)*
5. *Physics, or natural philosophy (chemistry, mineralogy)*
6. *Botany and zoology*
7. *Anatomy and medicine*
8. *Government, political economy, law of nature and nations, history, political law*
9. *Municipal law*
10. *Ideology, grammar, ethics, rhetoric, literature, fine arts*

Some of these disciplines grew out of the classical European tradition of learning—ancient languages, mathematics, natural philosophy, medicine, law. Other topics of study were new and American, like the modern languages, until then never studied seriously. The commissioners' report called Spanish "highly interesting," since it was "the language spoken by so great a portion of the inhabitants of our continents, with whom we shall probably have great intercourse ere long." In Anglo-Saxon, the commissioners were recommending the study of the English language, helpful as well for understanding common law. The arts were not traditionally considered objects of study at a university, and in fact the legislature omitted the fine arts when it carried out these recommendations.

It is equally interesting to note what branches of learning the commissioners did not recommend. "We have proposed no professor of divinity," their report states. Universal truths, "those in which all sects agree," may be taught through ethics and the ancient languages, but doctrinal matters specific to one sect or another they wished to "leave every sect to provide" outside the university. Within months critics attacked this aspect of the plan. Joseph Cabell called it "the Franklin that has drawn the lightning from the cloud of opposition."

As to discipline, the report questioned fear as a deterrent for youths of college age, and instead it proposed the affection between father and son as the model for faculty-student relations. If discipline is "founded in reason and comity," read the report, "it will be more likely to nourish in the minds of our youth the combined spirit of order and self-respect, so congenial with our political institutions, and so important to be woven into the American character." Seventy-nine-year-old Jefferson knew, though, that youth could take liberty too far. "Premature ideas of independence, too little repressed by parents," he wrote to a friend in 1822, "beget a spirit of insubordination which is the great obstacle to science with us and a principal cause of its decay since the revolution." Finding the balance—encouraging independence yet controlling insubordination among students—has remained a challenge throughout the history of the university.

My aim was to create for the young men a complete police of their own, tempered by the paternal affection of their tutors.

— *THOMAS JEFFERSON, 1816*

The Founding

Joseph C. Cabell, advocate for the university in the General Assembly

1825

- *123 students*

- *8 faculty members*

- *Tuition: $50 for one course of study; $60 for two; $75 for three*

- *Lawn and Range rooms: $15 per year*

Thomas Jefferson was determined that his new American university would open during his lifetime. In October 1823, the year in which he turned eighty, he wrote John Adams that he had found something to help him battle *tedium vitae*—the weariness of life: "I am fortunately mounted on a hobby, which, indeed, I should have better managed some thirty or forty years ago; but whose easy amble is still sufficient to give exercise and amusement to an octogenary rider. This is the establishment of a University." With such spirit he faced repeated challenges: lack of funding, paucity of local building materials, and the skepticism of fellow Virginians.

The Architecture of the University

Jefferson had been building the academical village in his imagination for years. Even during his presidency, in 1804, he had articulated the vision of "a plain small house for the school & lodging of each professor ... connected by covered ways out of which the rooms of the students should open." In fact, Jefferson wrote, "an University should not be an house but a village."

Jefferson shared his ideas with architects William Thornton and Benjamin Henry Latrobe. Latrobe, who had

Lawns and Ranges. *Early on, Jefferson envisioned walkways lined with small student rooms and larger faculty quarters. Joseph Cabell suggested the idea that evolved into the Lawns (two inner strings of rooms, facing inward) and the Ranges (two outer strings, facing outward), with gardens in between. Subsequent drawings enclosed the gardens within serpentine walls.*

A domed central building.
Writing on 24 July 1817 (below), Benjamin Henry Latrobe suggested a large domed central building for the university, including, as he wrote, "a circular lecture room inside the dome." Jefferson adopted Latrobe's idea immediately.

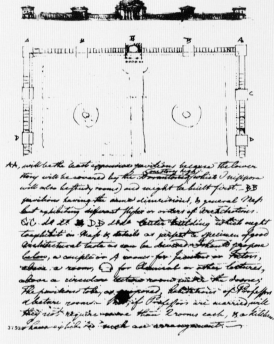

served as surveyor of public buildings and had designed the U.S. Capitol Building, suggested a focal domed building, larger than the adjacent pavilions. Having decided to create three terraces descending toward the Blue Ridge vista to the south, Jefferson wrote Latrobe that he planned to leave the north end open, "that if the state should establish there the University they contemplate, they may fill it up with something of the grand kind."

As Jefferson and Latrobe corresponded, the idea evolved that each pavilion should be different. They would present "models of taste and good architecture, and of a variety of appearance, no two alike, so as to serve as specimens for the Architectural lecturer." Each pavilion would represent "a distinct and different sample" of great architecture, following the neoclassical principles of the great Italian Renaissance architect Andrea Palladio, whom Jefferson had admired since his youth. Latrobe sent drawings, offering a variety of design possibilities. Jefferson adapted those suggestions and created final drawings of pavilion facades and floor plans.

Not until 1821 did the building at the head of the Lawn come to the

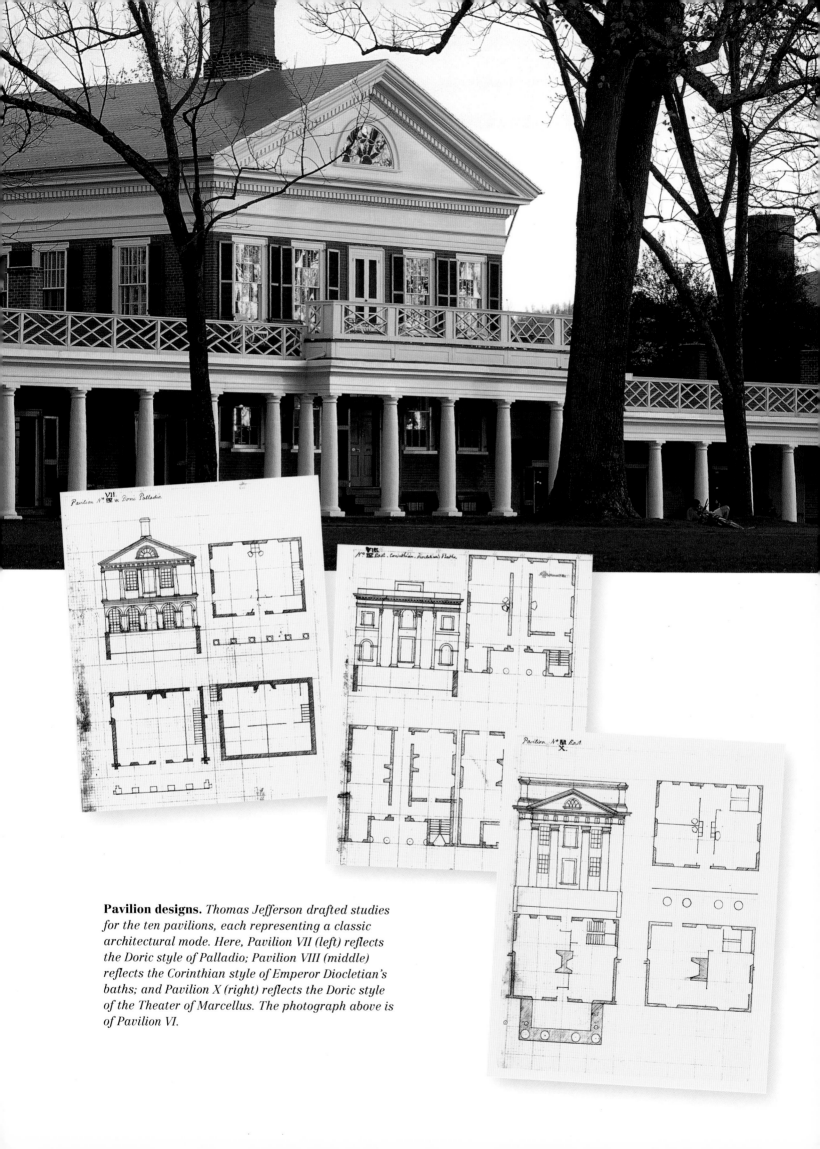

Pavilion designs. *Thomas Jefferson drafted studies for the ten pavilions, each representing a classic architectural mode. Here, Pavilion VII (left) reflects the Doric style of Palladio; Pavilion VIII (middle) reflects the Corinthian style of Emperor Diocletian's baths; and Pavilion X (right) reflects the Doric style of the Theater of Marcellus. The photograph above is of Pavilion VI.*

attention of the General Assembly as part of the plan—and part of the budget—for the university. The central building would be not a chapel, as at other colleges and academies, but a library. In his drawings, dating from 1819, Jefferson echoed in shape and splendor the Pantheon of Rome, which he had studied extensively through the work of Palladio. But Jefferson changed the form of the Pantheon for his purposes, conceiving a shape on paper within which a perfect circle could be inscribed.

By 1821 Jefferson could report to the university's Board of Visitors that six pavilions facing into the Lawn, two hotels facing out, and eighty-two student rooms had been completed, paid for by a $15,000 loan from the state's Literary Fund and subscribers' investments. Jefferson illustrated his report with a site plan,

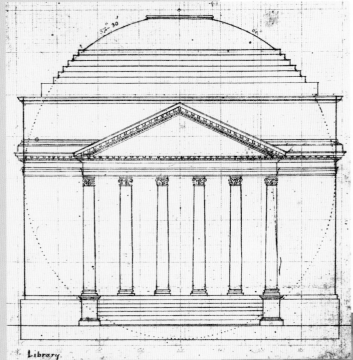

Geometric perfection, 1819. *To attain its pleasing dimensions, Jefferson raised his Rotunda above the ground floor, so that its architectural outline accommodated an inscribed circle. This matching pair of architectural drawings (left, below) showing the front façade and doorways of the Roman Pantheon appeared in Giacomo Leoni's famous 1742 volume on Palladio's architecture, which Jefferson studied.*

the first complete drawing since 1814. At its head he showed a hemispherical library building, divided into oval rooms, estimated to cost $42,000. Estimates for the rest of the academical village totaled about $195,000. In fact, by 1828, the cost for the residential buildings and the Rotunda had amounted to just less than $295,000.

Some legislators thought the Rotunda an unnecessary extravagance, but Jefferson considered it essential. "Had we built a barn for a college, and log huts for accommodations, should we ever have had the assurance to propose to an European professor ... to come to it?" he wrote Cabell. "To stop where we are is to abandon our high hopes, and become suitors to Yale and Harvard for their secondary characters." The more supportive 1823 legislature granted a $60,000 loan to complete all buildings, including the library.

In the Rotunda's design, Jefferson blended architectural ideas of the ages with his own innovative sense of space. He elevated his Rotunda fourteen

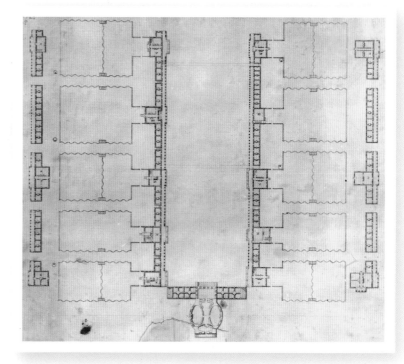

The Maverick plan, 1825. *John Neilson drafted and Peter Maverick engraved this ground plan of the university, which was printed in 1822 then revised in 1825 to include an arcade along the south front of the Rotunda. A copy of this plan was sold to prospective students.*

An early engraving. *Working from an 1824 drawing, Benjamin Tanner created this engraving, perhaps the earliest image of the complete academical village.*

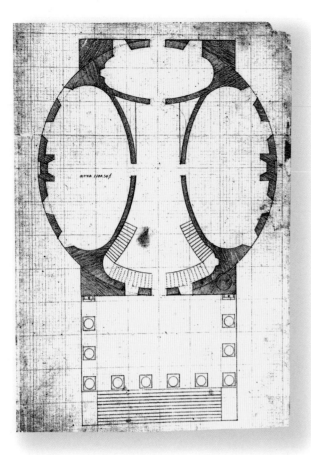

Floor plan of the Rotunda, 1823. *Probably drawn by Jefferson, this plan for the ground floor of the Rotunda included three distinctive oval-shaped rooms and a symmetrical staircase, resulting in graceful, sweeping interior lines throughout the building.*

steps above ground level, creating a sense of grandeur but maintaining balance with the pavilions on either side. He divided the inner space into two lower floors, each with three oval meeting rooms, and an upper floor—the Dome Room, round and open. Amid beauty, Jefferson always sought educational utility: he intended the Dome Room to be "painted sky-blue, and spangled with gilt stars" for use as a planetarium. He even designed a moving seat from which an operator could position the stars.

First Faculty

With the pavilions, dormitories, and Rotunda taking shape, the university needed also to establish a faculty. Jefferson summoned Francis Walker Gilmer, a thirty-four-year-old lawyer and son of his friend and physician, Dr. George Gilmer of Pen Park. He offered Francis Gilmer the position of professor of law but asked him first to travel to Europe as his emissary to convince other professors to come to

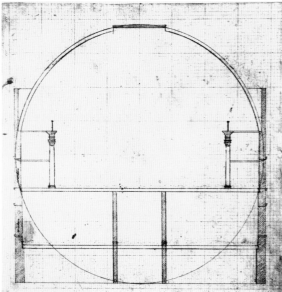

The Dome Room. *The third floor of Jefferson's Rotunda contained a single spherical room, ringed by a gallery atop twenty pairs of Corinthian columns. Jefferson wished the Dome Room to serve as a planetarium as well and designed a machine whereby a moving image of the starry sky could be projected onto the domed ceiling.*

Francis Walker Gilmer, recruiter of faculty. *Although offered a teaching position before leaving for Europe to recruit faculty, Gilmer did not at first accept. Jefferson attempted to hire a number of others and then returned to Gilmer, who agreed to join the faculty in the spring of 1826 but died before courses commenced. Thus, law was not offered as a course of study for the first year at the university, until John Tayloe Lomax, a Fredericksburg lawyer, joined the faculty.*

America. Gilmer visited Oxford, Cambridge, London, and Edinburgh, offering scholars who met his approval an annual salary of $1,000 to $1,500, a relatively low sum, augmented by a share of student fees and rent-free residence, with teaching to begin in February 1825.

Few of Gilmer's recruits managed to arrive by February. Five were detained on an "old log" of a boat, braving bad weather as they crossed the Atlantic. For a while, Jefferson feared them lost at sea. Finally, on 7 March 1825, the University of Virginia opened its doors to students, offering instruction under seven professors.

Criticism was leveled at Jefferson for having hired so many Europeans. Only Gilmer was American-born. Holding the chairs in natural philosophy and moral philosophy, John P. Emmet and George Tucker, although American citizens, were foreign-born; the others were European. For law and political science, Jefferson felt it important to hire an American. He left the choice of texts and topics to professors in other fields, but he and James Madison corresponded early on, creating a distinctly American reading list

University of Virginia.

Some Professors of the University, and of important branches of science, being not yet arrived, altho' they have been, for some time, hourly expected, the public are notified that as soon as they arrive, an early day will be fixed on for opening the Institution, and notice thereof published with such details of information as may be ~~necessary~~ necessary to be known to parents and students previous to entrance into the schools.

A. S. Brockenbrough Procto.

Th.J. to mr Brockenbrough.

I inclose you papers received from mr Coffee. I think it advisable to insert the above advertisement into the Enquirer and Constitutional whig of Richmond and the principal paper of Fredericksbg by the first mail to both places. it will be still in time to prevent students from coming on the 1st. of Feb. or before further notice. friendly salutations.

Jan. 9. 25.

University of Virginia.

In consideration of the delay which attended the opening of the University beyond the day on which it had been announced, the uncertainty which this might occasion in the minds of many at what time it might be opened, and the temporary engagements which, in consequence thereof, they might enter into elsewhere, Notice is given that, for the present year, Students will be received at the University at any time of the year when they may become disengaged, on payment of so much only of the usual charges as shall be proportioned to the time unexpired at the date of their reception.

A. S. B. Proctor of the University

to be published in the Central gazette, Enquirer & National Intelligencer.

in law and politics, which included the Declaration of Independence, the *Federalist Papers,* and Washington's inaugural address.

Jefferson had tried to recruit two Americans—George Ticknor, a scholar of Spanish literature at Harvard, and Nathaniel Bowditch, the great mathematician and navigator—but both declined. Jefferson came to believe that, given the small size of the American scholarly community, it was better for him to recruit overseas, "preferring foreigners of the first order to natives of the second," as he wrote to John Adams in 1819. Competition between the university and Harvard had begun even before the university opened. George Ticknor wrote Jefferson that at Harvard, "we shall never become what we might be easily unless we are led or driven to it by a rival," and that there was "no immediate prospect of such a rival except in your University."

Notice of delayed opening. *When in early January 1825 the university was not yet ready to open, Thomas Jefferson corresponded with the university proctor, A. S. Brockenbrough, to compose an announcement of the delay, which was placed in Charlottesville's* Central Gazette, Richmond's Enquirer, *and Washington's* National Intelligencer.

The First Faculty

Dunglison

Emmet

Bonnycastle

Long

Tucker

Key

Robley Dunglison, professor of anatomy and medicine. *Originally from the Lake District, Dunglison studied widely throughout Europe and was practicing medicine in London when recruited. His eminence was recognized here quickly, with Yale awarding him an honorary degree in 1825. During Jefferson's last months, Dunglison attended him as personal physician, as he did also James Madison and Andrew Jackson. While at the university, Dunglison produced several medical works, including a famous medical dictionary and a text on human physiology. He lived in Pavilion X.*

John P. Emmet, professor of natural history. *Although originally from Ireland, Emmet was one of two American citizens on the faculty. Emmet attended West Point and was a popular lecturer in chemistry in Charleston, South Carolina, before coming to the university. Emmet kept pet snakes, an owl, and a bear in Pavilion I until his new bride, niece of faculty member George Tucker, protested. He moved from the Lawn and built Morea, on today's Sprigg Lane, where he cultivated mulberries and silkworms.*

Charles Bonnycastle, professor of natural philosophy. *Bonnycastle, son of a noted English mathematician, wrote treatises on algebra and geometry, and he became professor of mathematics when Thomas Key returned to England. An expert in trigonometry, he was said to be intensely shy and abstracted. He arrived a bachelor but married a Loudoun County woman and had three children, and he was known to grow roses and honeysuckle in their garden behind Pavilion VI.*

George Long, professor of ancient languages. *The youngest of the faculty, Long impressed Jefferson as "acquiring esteem as fast as he becomes known." He lived in Pavilion V, and in his first year he married the university proctor's daughter. While on the faculty, he contributed to a book on etymology and collaborated with Robley Dunglison on their* Introduction to the Study of Grecian and Roman Geography. *Long returned to his native England in 1828. In later years he referred to himself as "an unreconstructed rebel," and he wrote a tribute to Robert E. Lee in his translation of Marcus Aurelius.*

George Tucker, professor of moral philosophy. *Born in Bermuda, Tucker attended the College of William and Mary and served on Virginia's General Assembly. He was a U.S. congressman when invited to the university. Known for his writing, from essays on taste and politics to novels—including* A Voyage to the Moon, *considered to be America's first work of interplanetary science fiction— Tucker later wrote a biography of Jefferson and a four-volume history of the United States. He lived in Pavilion IX and taught ethics, logic, and statistics.*

Thomas Hewett Key, professor of mathematics. *Key studied mathematics at Trinity College, Cambridge, and trained in medicine in London. While at the University of Virginia, he began a lifelong study of Latin, which culminated in his later writing a major dictionary of Latin. He stayed only two years in Virginia, returning to England. He and his wife lived in Pavilion VIII.*

The Father of the University

More than any other university in America, and perhaps in the world, the University of Virginia bears the impress of its founder. Thomas Jefferson envisioned his university intellectually; he drafted, surveyed, chose materials, and oversaw construction. He spent months developing the acquisitions list of almost seven thousand books, the core of the library collections. He was also a familiar part of students' lives in those early years. It is said that every Sunday evening four or five students would dine with him at Monticello. Those whose religion barred them from a Sunday outing he invited on a weekday, ultimately hosting every student at his home.

Thomas Jefferson knew that the creation of the University of Virginia would be the last of his many momentous accomplishments. In a sense, it culminated his life's work, bringing ideas, design, and social vision together into one creation. He died on 4 July 1826. While the cannons boomed to celebrate Independence Day, the courthouse bell began tolling as well, announcing the death of the Sage of Monticello, according to a later account in a Charlottesville newspaper. Jefferson's funeral, "modest and unpretending as he had directed," according to George Tucker, was conducted in the rain. After squabbling over who should lead the procession, citizens of Charlottesville and students of the university trekked up the mountain to Monticello, arriving too late to see the casket placed into the earth. At the site was erected a tombstone, on which Jefferson wished only three accomplishments recorded: that he had written the Declaration of Independence and the Statute for Religious Freedom in Virginia and, finally, that he had been not the founder but the "Father of the University of Virginia."

George Blaetterman, professor of modern languages. *Blaetterman could teach French, German, Spanish, Italian, Danish, Swedish, Dutch, Portuguese, and Anglo-Saxon. Described by Jefferson as "rather a rough-looking German," he caused consternation among faculty in 1835 by painting the front of Pavilion IV (above), where he lived until 1840, when he was dismissed by the Board of Visitors for "the violence said to have been recently and publicly inflicted by him on the person of Mrs. Blaetterman."*

At *[Jefferson's] last visit to the*
university, only a few weeks be-
fore his death, as I was informed
by the late William Wertenbaker,
he stood at the window in front
of the Library Room, looking
out upon the Lawn, until
Mr. Wertenbaker brought him
a chair from his own office,
when he sat for twenty minutes
or so, watching the lifting of
the first marble capital to the
top of its pillar, the one at
the southwest corner. This
concluded, he left the grounds
and never returned.

— PROFESSOR FRANCIS H. SMITH

THE LAWN

An aerial perspective displays the symmetry and symbolism of Thomas Jefferson's university, an "academical village" of students and faculty, living and learning together. Student rooms, intended by Jefferson as doubles but now used as singles, attach to faculty quarters and classrooms by shady colonnades. Today residence on the East and West Lawn is granted to students chosen by their faculty and peers as academic and community leaders. The accommodations may appear primitive (with working fireplaces and distant bathrooms), but students consider it a privilege to live on the Lawn.

Lawn rooms connect to ten pavilions, designed by Jefferson to accommodate faculty living upstairs and classes downstairs. Distances between the pavilions are not equal: those closer to the Rotunda are closer to one another. Jefferson may have chosen these dimensions to highlight the perspective of the view to the Rotunda, but the terraced landscape may also simply have required this design.

Jefferson's educational ideals directed the architecture of his pavilions. He envisioned ten fields of study and ten professors at his university; for years after its founding, each pavilion was devoted to a given subject, and its tenure passed along to each succeeding professor in the field. Today, faculty live in nine of the pavilions. The tenth, Pavilion VII, where the Lawn's first cornerstone was laid, served as the library until the Rotunda opened. From 1907 on, Pavilion VII has housed the Colonnade Club, a guest hotel.

Between the Lawn and the Ranges stretch ten gardens, some divided in two. The serpentine walls enclosing these gardens were designed by Jefferson after

The Lawn, ca. 1965. Right: fencers at the serpentine walls, ca. 1930.

English "crinkle-crankle walls," whose combination of strength, efficiency of materials, and beauty he admired.

In the early years of the university, fruits and vegetables were probably grown in some of these gardens as food for faculty and students. Livestock grazed right outside the university bounds and sometimes found their way through garden gates, wreaking havoc on the harvest. Between 1948 and 1965, the Garden Club of Virginia reconstructed the gardens of the university grounds. Each garden follows a distinctive pattern, some highly formal and others more natural in design.

Many intriguing botanical specimens are cultivated in the university gardens, including flowers and trees known to have interested Jefferson. An early column capital of Virginia stone, which proved unsuitable for use in the Rotunda, can be found in the garden behind Pavilion I. A spire from Merton College Chapel, Oxford, stands in the garden behind Pavilion VI. Originally carved in 1451, the chapel spires were removed for safekeeping during World War I. This one, given to the University of Virginia as a token of academic fellowship, was rebuilt on the university grounds in 1928.

Jefferson designed one other building for his university: the Anatomical Theater, constructed after his death. This blocky, two-story building with high, lunette windows stood beyond the West Range. In it, medical students sat in an amphitheater, watching surgery professors perform dissections. Burned out and then restored in the 1880s, the Anatomical Theater was torn down in 1938 to make room for Alderman Library.

In the early 1960s, architecture professors Frederick D. Nichols and William B. O'Neal initiated the public discussion of historic accuracy in the restoration of the Rotunda. At the same time, the architecture school at the university had just begun to offer groundbreaking courses in historic preservation. In 1979 the decision was made to offer not a separate degree but a certificate in historic preservation as part of a traditional architecture degree. Virginia also became the first American university to offer a degree in architectural history.

In 1984, just after the Rotunda had been restored to its Jeffersonian design, the university embarked on a forty-year plan to restore the rest of the academical village. Generous private donations during the capital campaign of the 1990s supported,

A column capital of Virginia stone, discarded by Jefferson, now in the garden of Pavilion I

for example, the restoration of Pavilion VII, preserving historic features, updating amenities, and furnishing and decorating it in keeping with its Jeffersonian past.

In the many decisions he must make during each phase of the restoration, architect F. Murray Howard, curator of the academical village, seeks a balance between historic accuracy and current utility. "This is not a museum," says Howard. "It's a living property. If we undermine that by freezing any part of it, we have done a disservice to the early concept of the academical village."

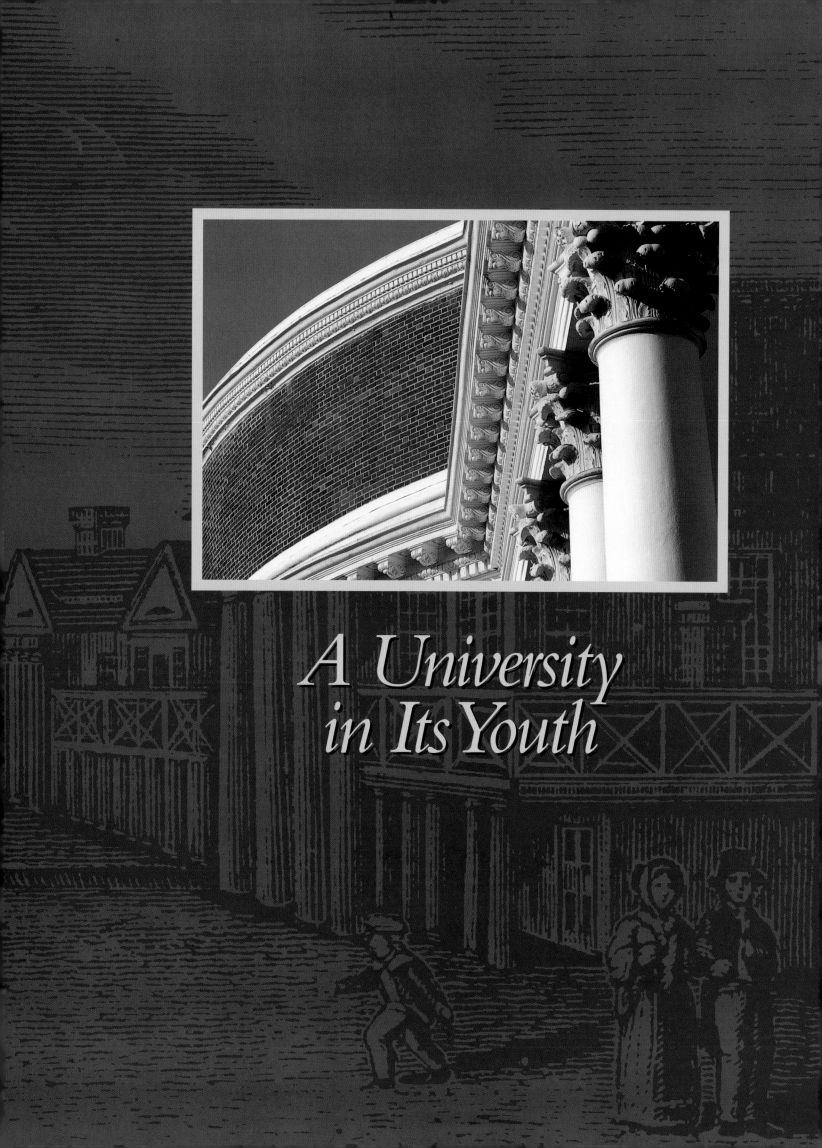

A University
in Its Youth

James Madison,
second rector
of the university

1840

- **180 students**

- **11 faculty members**

- **Tuition: $50 for one course of study; $60 for two; $75 for three**

- **Lawn and Range rooms: $16 per year**

- **Pocket money, no more than $40 annually, deposited with the bursar**

- **Dark gray cloth for uniforms cost up to $6 a yard**

- **The Collegian, ten issues annually, cost $2.50 per year**

By February 1826 the university's 109 dormitory rooms were full. For a year's residence, a young man paid fifteen dollars, which secured not only a shared room but also housekeeping services. Students were forbidden to bring "servant, dog or horse" with them to the university, but records suggest that the university owned slaves in those early years. Tasks expected of these "servants" were set forth in the minutes of an 1842 meeting of the Board of Visitors. They were to bring water and towels, make the beds, and clean the rooms of students daily; clean the candlesticks and black the andirons weekly; and wash windows once a month. Every afternoon they were also expected to black the shoes of students.

The janitor rang the morning bell before dawn. If students ignored it, he roused them bodily. Students breakfasted in hotels by candlelight and then, according to their course of study, attended classes throughout the day.

Each school, representing a different field of study, offered classes during a two-hour block three times a week:

MWF 7:30–9:30 A.M. School of ancient languages, offering advanced Latin and Greek, Hebrew, rhetoric, belles lettres, ancient history, and ancient geography

TThS 7:30–9:30 A.M. School of modern languages, offering French, Spanish, Italian, German, Anglo-Saxon, modern history, and modern geography

MWF 9:30–11:30 A.M. School of mathematics, offering advanced numerical arithmetic, algebra, trigonometry, plane and spherical

The first student. *Because his was the first name written in the matriculation book (shown at right), Burwell Starke (above) of Hanover County, Virginia, is considered the first student at the university. He became a merchant and farmer in Dover, Missouri, and lived until 1895.*

geometry, mensuration, navigation, conic sections, fluxions or differentials, military and civil architecture

TThS 9:30–11:30 A.M. *School of natural philosophy, offering mechanics, statics, hydrostatics, hydraulics, pneumatics, acoustics, optics, and astronomy*

MWF 11:30 A.M.–1:30 P.M. *School of natural history, offering botany, zoology, mineralogy, chemistry, geology, and rural economy*

TThS 11:30 A.M.–1:30 P.M. *School of anatomy and medicine, offering anatomy, surgery, history and theory of medicine, physiology, pathology, materia medica, and pharmacy*

MWF 1:30–3:30 P.M. *School of moral philosophy, offering ideology, general grammar, logic, and ethics*

TThS 1:30–3:30 P.M. *School of law, offering common, statute, chancery, feudal, civil, mercatorial, and maritime law and the law of nature and nations, government, and political economy*

On Saturday afternoons, all students participated in military training, which involved "field evolutions, manoeuvres and encampments."

The university did not require a set course of study but rather offered many subjects from which a student could choose. To give students such freedom was a new idea, and educators saw the University of Virginia as a risky experiment. The only required subject was Latin. "If he be also a proficient in the Greek, let that, too, be stated in his diploma," stated university regulations, since "proficiency in these languages . . . constitute[s] the basis of good education, and [is] indispensable to fill up the character of a 'well-educated man.'" Students paid fifty dollars to study one subject, sixty for two, twenty-five apiece for three or more—although by 1829 they were required to enroll in at least three subjects to earn a diploma. Students could attend religious services outside the university as long as they returned to "meet their school in the University at its stated hour."

University professors of the time customarily taught by recitation: that is, they read aloud from textbooks, which were so dear that students could not own their own copies. But at Jefferson's university, freedom of thought and rigor of argument were highly valued, and professors were encouraged to instruct "by lessons or lectures, examinations and exercises, as shall be best adapted to the nature of the science, and number of the

school." Students received further exercises "to employ the vacant days and hours."

Because of the high cost of printed material in those early years, library rules were restrictive. Faculty had access, but students could borrow books only with a professor's permission. Only twenty students, admitted by tickets, could enter the library per day. Fines for late returns were based on the size of the book in question.

In this institution there is no curriculum or prescribed course of study.... In establishing the University of Virginia, Mr. Jefferson, for the first time in America, threw open the doors of a University in the true sense of the name, ... allowing students to select for themselves the departments to which they are led by their special tastes.

— *UNIVERSITY OF VIRGINIA CATALOGUE, 1881*

William Wertenbaker, early librarian. *The university librarian from 1826 through 1881, Wertenbaker was characterized as strict and decorous. He could recall from memory the whereabouts—or borrower—of every library book and pamphlet. The last surviving university staff member to have known Jefferson personally, he shared many reminiscences of the founding years with later students.*

Reading room privileges. *In the early nineteenth century, a student had to purchase a ticket to visit the university library and peruse its books. In the late nineteenth century, a student paid two dollars a session to use the reading rooms in the Rotunda.*

Student's Reading Rooms,
UNIVERSITY OF VIRGINIA.
189__-'9__
Mr. *Jas. A. Turner*
The holder of this ticket, having paid the fee of $2.00, is entitled to the use of the rooms during the session, under the
PLEDGE
never to take out of the rooms or to mutilate any periodical or book. ☞ NOT TRANSFERABLE.

SHOW THIS TICKET TO THE SUPERINTENDENT.

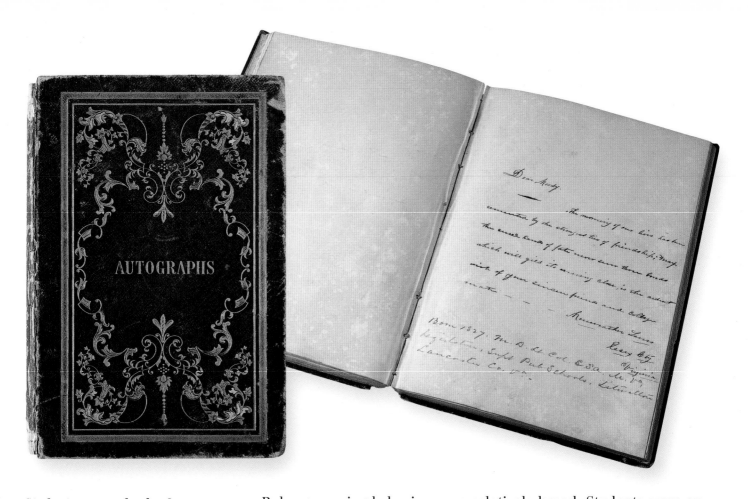

Student memory books. *In the 1850s and 1860s, students purchased autograph albums containing an essay about the University of Virginia and imprinted throughout with engravings or lithographs of its faculty members. Students wrote each other sentimental inscriptions, like this one to William Moody from a student named Meriwether Lewis (not the man sent by Jefferson across the continent).*

Rules governing behavior were relatively broad. Students were exhorted not to engage in "habits of expense, of dissoluteness, dissipation, or of playing at games of chance." Only with permission from a professor might students "make any festive entertainment." The playing of musical instruments was acceptable, but otherwise students were to make no "disturbing noises," including firing guns or pistols. "Riotous, disorderly, intemperate or indecent conduct" would result in eviction from university residence. "Fighting with weapons which may inflict death" resulted in "instant expulsion from the University, not remissible by the Faculty." Major offenses would be tried and punished by the faculty, while minor offenses were to be referred to "a board of six censors, to be named by the faculty, from the most discreet of the students"—an early expression of the principle that students should police themselves, as later instituted in an honor system. Civil offenses would be referred directly to the local magistrate.

The school year opened in February and lasted to the fifteenth of December, when "highly meritorious" students appeared for public examinations in an oval room of the Rotunda. Students "of highest qualification" received diplomas, a second tier received medals, and a third received books. Students could consider themselves graduates of the university after a year of classes. The first commencement exercises were held in 1829, at

Medical diploma, 1833. *When William G. Carr received his diploma in medicine, it was signed by George Tucker, chairman of the faculty; by Robley Dunglison and John P. Emmet, professors of medicine and chemistry; and by Thomas Johnson, demonstrator of anatomy and surgery.*

a "Public Day" in the Rotunda, at which names of students receiving honors were read and five students delivered orations.

Debating Societies

As at other young American colleges, students at the University of Virginia quickly formed literary, or debating, societies, which met for the sport of argumentation and were, according to historian James McLachlan, "colleges within colleges," with their own governments and calendars. The first such group at Virginia called itself the Patrick Henry Society—an ironic identification, as university historian Philip A. Bruce points out, given Thomas Jefferson's antipathy to the Federalist orator. Two groups established in this early era survive to the present day: the Jefferson Debating and Literary Society (considered the earliest extant student organization, established in 1825) and the Washington Literary Society (established around 1835).

At weekly or fortnightly meetings, members of debating societies engaged in rhetorical jousting over topics of local or national interest. Subjects of debate could be abstract and theoretical—such as the origins of language—or immediate and political—on emancipation, for instance. Each society staged special anniversary celebrations, involving ceremonial readings from Washington's farewell address or the Declaration of Independence and oratorical performances by speakers selected for the occasion. One such student, Richard Parker, who addressed the Jefferson Society on 4 July 1833, entered Congress and ultimately presided at the trial of John Brown in 1859.

Early student magazine. *Students founded literary magazines in the early years of the university, in part because the curriculum did not include courses in writing. Lengthy articles treated serious academic subjects, including the question of whether America could develop its own literary tradition.*

Edgar Allan Poe, the university's first literary son. *At the age of seventeen, Poe attended the university for less than a year during its second session, from February to December 1826. Biographers have tried to find seeds of his later despair in his year at the university, but those who knew him insisted he was not prone to drink and only occasionally to gamble. Poe served as secretary of the Jefferson Debating Society and addressed that group on the subject of "Heat and Cold." Unable to pay fees, Poe borrowed, then gambled, and ultimately left the university two thousand dollars in debt, claiming he "became dissolute" because his uncle had sent him to university without enough to live on.*

Poe's Room, 13 West Range. *Renovated in the twentieth century as a historic display, this room gives a sense of daily student life in the university's first years. Poe lived on the West Range, perhaps in this room.*

Student Rowdiness

Within months of opening the university to students in March 1825, Jefferson was complaining of their "incipient irregularities." By fall, trouble erupted. According to George Tucker, chairman of the faculty, "nightly disorders were habitual with the students," and on 1 October 1825, "they reached a point of riot and excess." Masked students ran whooping across the Lawn and attacked two professors who were trying to quiet them down. When the faculty demanded to know the rioters' identity, students banded together in silence. The Board of Visitors summoned them to the Rotunda. Henry Tutwiler, a student in those days, later recalled that Jefferson "began by saying that this was the most painful event of his life, but soon became so much affected that he could not proceed." Visitor Chapman Johnson took over the proceedings, and ultimately fourteen volunteered their identities. After questioning, three were expelled, including Wilson Miles Cary, Jefferson's own kin, the great-grandson of his sister Martha and his dear friend Dabney Carr.

"The shock which Mr. Jefferson felt," Tucker wrote in his *Life of Thomas Jefferson,* "when he for the first time discovered that the efforts of the last ten years of his life had been foiled and put in jeopardy by one of his family, was more than his own patience could endure, and he could not forbear from using, for the first time, the language of indignation and reproach." Following this action, masks and disguises were outlawed; "profane swearing" was deemed a crime; "contumacy" was recategorized from a minor to a major offense.

Reacting to those who refused to incriminate their fellow students, the visitors also articulated the Jeffersonian principles that would ultimately form the core of the University of Virginia's honor code. "The Visitors are aware that a prejudice prevails too extensively among the young that it is dishonorable to bear witness one against another. . . . But this loose principle in the ethics of school-boy combinations, is unworthy of mature and regulated minds," they wrote. "Certainly, where wrong has been done, he

Stylish southern gentlemen. *During the university's first decade, faculty strove to enforce a uniform law. The dress code had been rescinded by 1850, the date of the photograph opposite, the earliest known group portrait of University of Virginia students. David Hunter Strother, the artist who (under the pseudonym Porte Crayon) sketched this 1853 caricature of a University of Virginia student (above), commented that "although the vivacity of these blooded colts at the University frequently leads them into all sorts of deviltries and excesses, they have almost invariably the manners of gentlemen."*

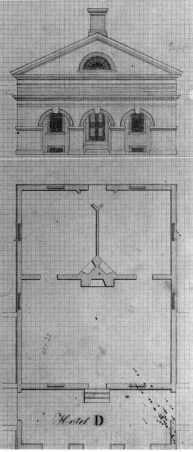

Hotels on the Ranges. *While pavilions for faculty housing were built among student rooms facing onto the Lawn, hotels for student dining were built facing out. At right, Jefferson's drawing for Hotel D on the West Range. Since then the hotels and the suite of rooms attached to the Rotunda in later years (above) have served as homes, offices, classrooms, and gathering places for staff, faculty, and students. For a time Hotel F even served as a gymnasium.*

who knows and conceals the doer of it, makes himself an accomplice, and justly censurable as such." The "good and the virtuous" ought to single out "the disorderly" for the sake of the institution.

For many years to come, though, in the spring or in the fall, students would conjure up a "calathump," as these rowdy demonstrations came to be called. The university librarian John S. Patton, in a turn-of-the-century account, wrote that even into the 1850s, "Masked students paraded the grounds, fired their revolvers, and made the night hideous to those who remained indoors and dangerous to those who ventured out." In 1825 masked students, crying "Down with the European professors!," focused their attacks on Professors Long and Key (who resigned their posts and returned to England within the year). In 1831 students swarmed a faculty meeting, this time apparently in protest of the recently required uniform—pantaloons, vest, and gray single-breasted waistcoat with a stiff, braided collar. Faculty, despite the founding principles of least government possible, imposed more and more controls upon the student body in an attempt to mold it into respectability.

Living conditions at the university may partly explain student unrest. Heat (provided by firewood) and light (by either candles or oil) were often in short supply and rather expensive. Sanitation was primitive at best. Typhoid and cholera swept through often, sometimes killing students. Some suspected that university quarters even spawned disease, with no clinic in which to treat, no infirmary in which to quarantine stricken students. The food offered at the hotels was often meager and unpalatable. The hotel keepers—private businessmen thrust into a guardianship position—sometimes hosted drinking and gambling in the evening hours.

In the fall of 1836, students rioted again, this time over their right to maintain a military company—with muskets. The faculty demanded students turn in their firearms; students refused. Faculty searched student dormitories for arms, and when the faculty announced their decision to expel the offenders, the military unit raised its ensign atop the Rotunda and shot the flag to shreds. Professors and their families feared for their safety. After three days the sheriff was called, and the Rotunda was placed under military guard. Although some urged stiffer discipline, faculty chairman John A. G. Davis argued that any student should be allowed to return to the fold provided he either "disclaim" participation or make "proper atonement."

Students commemorated the riot of November 1836 annually. In 1840, the calathumping went too far. A student of the time, Hunter Marshall, described events in a letter to a friend. Two of his classmates, he wrote, "disguised themselves with much secrecy as if they premeditated some dark deed" and "marched forth on the lawn with their pistols which with the assistance of their voices they succeeded in making much noise." Professor Davis—who had so magnanimously forgiven students in 1836—stepped outside his door at Pavilion X and attempted to unmask one of the rioters.

John A. G. Davis, second professor of law. *In politics a disciple of Jefferson and Madison, Davis was an influential member of the faculty. Although the object of pranks (students trimmed the tail of his horse down to the nub, for example), Davis still argued that the university should not expel any rabblerouser who turned in his musket and expressed regret for his misdeeds. When he stepped outside Pavilion X (above) on the night of 12 November 1840, investigating yet another student row, Davis was shot and killed.*

Gessner Harrison, professor of ancient languages, recounted the story this way: "Professor Davis in the vigor of health, and in the meridian of life, was shot down before his own door-sill in the wantonness of ruffian malice, when he had no suspicion of danger, was without the means of injury or defence, and when his only provocation was an unsuccessful attempt to discover who had disturbed his domestic peace and violated the laws of the University." The guilty student, identified as "Joseph Sems from Georgia" in Marshall's letter, was jailed and released under five thousand dollars bond. He never returned for trial and was rumored to have died soon thereafter, perhaps by suicide.

The Call to Honor

Sobered by Professor Davis's murder, students, faculty, and visitors "wore the badge of mourning for sixty days" and sought to regain order at the university. The record is silent about interactions during the next months, but by 2 July 1842, the faculty approved a resolution expressing trust in the students and implicitly harking back to Jefferson's own principle that the least government was the best.

"Resolved," the faculty recorded, "That in all future written examinations for distinction or other honors of the University each candidate shall attach to the written answers presented by him on such examination a certificate in the following words—'I, A. B., do hereby certify on honor that I have derived no assistance during the time of this examination from any source whatever, either oral written or in print giving the above answers."

Although the language of the pledge has undergone revision over the years, the spirit of this proposal still prevails at the University of Virginia. Students sign an honor pledge on every examination and term paper, stating that "On my honor as a student, I have neither given nor received assistance." Other aspects of the honor system, such as student-run trials with the power to force expulsion, developed much later. Nevertheless, in the words of the turn-of-the-century faculty chairman William M. Thornton, after Davis's death, "a nobler tradition grew up in the student body." It may not have meant an end to all calathumping, but it did mean the beginning of a new ethic of student behavior.

HONOR

In the early years of the university, there was no honor code, no system, no pledge. Honor existed at the University of Virginia as part of the culture of the southern gentleman. A man developed his character and built a reputation of forthright behavior; no less was expected of him. Thomas Jefferson elevated this ethic into a philosophy of education, which "improves what in [human] nature was vicious and perverse into qualities of virtue and social worth," as he expressed in the Rockfish Gap Commission report. His contemporary biographer George Tucker wrote that Jefferson "allowed more latitude and indulgence to students than was usual" and attempted to create a community where order was enforced "by appeals to their reason, their hopes, and to every generous feeling, rather than to the fear of punishment, or dread of disgrace."

The enactments of the university created a student "board of censors," but students at first were not inclined to incriminate one another. When in 1841 a group of students was arrested for drunken disorderliness, the

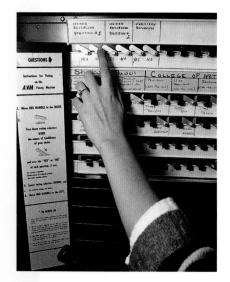

In frequent referenda from the 1970s on, students voted to uphold the honor code and its single sanction.

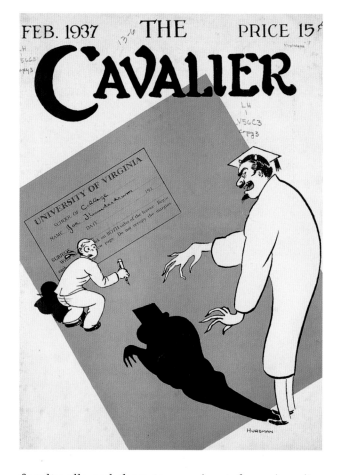

faculty allowed them to remain at the university, granted that for each wrongdoer three other students signed a pledge promising to report further misbehavior. That decision established a precedent. For the next few years faculty used the technique of appointing "sureties"—fellow students assigned to oversee those who had misbehaved—as a way to shape a self-policing culture.

Students took pride in an unspoken code that assumed them to be honorable and honest. In 1860 the student magazine described the University of Virginia as one of the only institutions in the country where order came through the "internal force" of gentility rather than by laws imposed from without, "presuming on the want of gentility and morality in the students." It was the spirit, not the wording, of pledges that mattered. One early alumnus simply wrote on his examination, "Perfectly fair on my part." In 1907 William Thornton told of an alumnus of the 1830s who addressed students late in the nineteenth century. The aged visitor "told as a merry jest the tale of some petty examination-cheatery, which he had himself committed in his student days. The crowded banquet room was silent as the grave. . . . The younger alumni looked as if dumb with disbelief."

Many have considered that the murder of John A. G. Davis by a student in 1840 triggered the creation of the university's honor system. In fact, the cornerstone of the system, the examination pledge, was proposed two years later by Henry St. George Tucker, the law professor who succeeded Davis. Early faculty had gone to great lengths to proctor students writing examinations. Tucker suggested, however, that students would live up to faculty expectations and recommended that students sign

The Senff Memorial Gates, built in 1912 as a tribute to the honor system

every examination with a pledge of honor. With faculty approval, students began shouldering the responsibility for classroom honesty. The honor pledge remained essentially the same into and through the twentieth century, ultimately refined to the simpler phrase, "On my honor as a student, I have neither given nor received aid on this examination."

In 1909 the *College Topics* newspaper reported on the "machinery" of the honor system, perfected through discussion among students that spring. According to what came to be called the Code of 1909,

a student who believed he had witnessed a breach of honor was to, with other classmates if he desired, investigate the matter secretly and speedily, then "demand of the accused an explanation of his conduct." The accused was either to leave school or, if he wished to defend himself, to contact the president of his class, asking for a trial before the honor committee, made up of student presidents from university departments plus the vice president from the accused's department. Other students could attend the trial if the accused so desired. Students could

After 1842, professors trusted students to be honest on examinations. Above, a professor's drafted exam concludes with the expected student pledge.

serve as counsel on either side. A vote of five out of six honor committee members would result in expulsion, at which point "the accused must leave college immediately."

Early twentieth-century honor committees decided to list possible offenses explicitly. "The honor system concerns itself not only with examinations but with drinking, gambling, pledges made to the Faculty, contests for honors in the Literary Societies—with nearly every student relationship into which lying or cheating may enter," read a pamphlet published around 1912. In this era the dance pledge was instated, whereby a student attending an evening party pledged that he had not had a drink since before that noon. Athletes took a similar pledge of sobriety before going onto the playing field.

Faculty helped raise discussions of honor to a higher plane through their annual orientation lecture to students, delivered by some of the most revered professors during the mid-twentieth century. In 1932 the law professor George P. Eager explained to new students that the university's honor system was "in essence a *spirit* and not a code, remaining always as elastic as the student body's conception of the honor of a gentleman may be at any given stage of evolution." In 1952 the political science professor Stringfellow Barr reminded students of the "deep reciprocal relations between the act of telling the truth and the act of seeking with faith to know what is true"—in other words, the intellectual work of the university. "Right action and aesthetic beauty will not survive where clear strong thinking fails," added Barr. In 1976, reflecting that "we are now 15,000 students spread from the Law School on the North Grounds to the Alderman Road dorms to the Medical School to Lambeth Field, and indeed all over Albemarle County," the law professor Daniel J. Meador called the honor system "the mortar which holds the bricks together [and] a common bond uniting all."

Ideally, the honor system brought students together, but the system raised conflict as well. Before coeducation, some male students doubted whether women and men could regard each other equally under an honor system. As the university was integrated, critics noted that proportionately more African American students were accused of honor offenses. The student press and law students played critical roles in the evolution of the system. Debates arose over the relative "reprehensibility" of honor offenses. In 1975 the student newspaper, the *Cavalier Daily,* published the full transcript of an honor trial, before considered confidential. By that time law students served as counsel to the accused, but in 1983 they threatened to secede and create a law school honor system on their own.

Students repeatedly voted to uphold the system, expressing faith in its ideals. In 1996 the honor committee abbreviated its regulations, seeking clarity and precision. Interpretation changed from generation to generation, bringing debate—and through such debate, continued engagement in the principles of honor.

Thomas Barclay, attending the university in its first two sessions, wrote this request for leniency from the Board of Visitors, who adjudicated cases of serious misconduct before the student-run honor system began. His request was denied.

War,
Reconstruction,
and Fire

Thomas Jefferson Randolph, Thomas Jefferson's grandson and seventh rector of the university

By the late 1850s the university enjoyed a reputation as "the pride of Virginia" and "the recognized head of Southern colleges," according to student comments published in the university's literary magazine. Students came largely from the agrarian gentry of the South—not only from Virginia, but also, especially, from Alabama, Louisiana, and Kentucky. A student was either an "Academ," a "Med," or a "Law," enrolled in the academical, the medical, or the law department. Enrollment had grown to over six hundred, thus all-university events could no longer be held inside the Rotunda. Classroom space was inadequate as well. Five schools—ancient and modern languages, mathematics, moral philosophy, and law—shared two lecture halls for all of their classes. With Thomas Jefferson Randolph, Jefferson's grandson, as rector, the university decided to build an annex to the Rotunda.

The job of designing the Rotunda Annex went to Robert Mills, a renowned public architect and designer of the Washington Monument, who had worked as a draftsman for both Jefferson and Latrobe. Mills proposed a building "150 feet long including Porticoes, and 50 feet wide, which from the declivity of the ground, will afford 4 large lecture rooms, a large exhibition

1880

- **600 students**

- **22 faculty members**

- **Tuition: $25 for one course of study, usually totaling $75**

- **Expenses: $97 annually for rent, fuel and lights, washing, and library and infirmary fees**

- **Boardinghouse rent: $15 per month**

The expanded Rotunda. *As the student population outgrew the original academical village, the Annex was added to the Rotunda, stretching 150 feet north and containing classrooms and the large Public Hall.*

room and museum above, all accessible from the Rotunda, from which it is separated by a colonnaded space." The view from the portico, he promised, "will be magnificent."

It may be hard to imagine today why anyone would add an annex to Jefferson's Rotunda, but the modern sense of awe over Jefferson's academical village was not shared by all in the nineteenth century. Students complained that, instead of the "noble statuary, stately trees, beautiful pleasure

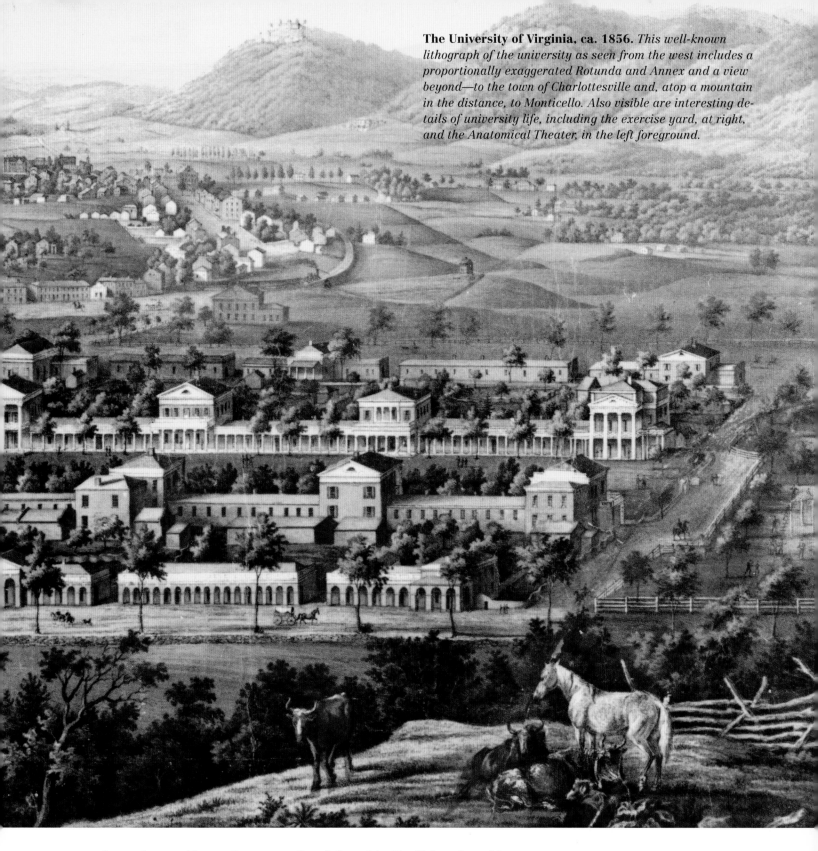

The University of Virginia, ca. 1856. *This well-known lithograph of the university as seen from the west includes a proportionally exaggerated Rotunda and Annex and a view beyond—to the town of Charlottesville and, atop a mountain in the distance, to Monticello. Also visible are interesting details of university life, including the exercise yard, at right, and the Anatomical Theater, in the left foreground.*

grounds, and magnificent flower gardens" found in English universities, at the University of Virginia "we have an occasional dingy lamp-post, a sickly locust, a good sized common for the Charlottesville cows."

Some called Mills's Annex "splendid." It opened to the north, where in 1858 a new road allowed carriages to "drive up and deposit their load under the building just in the rear of the Rotunda." Before, traffic circled around the south end of the Lawn. "*Ladies* especially," the student

The Public Hall. *Here, decorated for the 1867 Founder's Day celebrations, is the new Public Hall, built on the second floor of the Annex and designed to accommodate a larger student body. Behind the podium hung a copy of Raphael's School of Athens, purchased for the university through alumni donations and dedicated in 1857. Originally created by Raphael in 1510, the painting portrays Plato, Socrates, and fellow philosophers.*

magazine announced, "will not be forced to walk a long distance in the open air." Attached by wooden beams to the Rotunda, the Annex did seem to some a fire hazard. Rector Randolph "said it would be the cause of the destruction of the Rotunda, as it was!" wrote the librarian John S. Patton, one of hundreds who watched in 1895 as fire spread from the Annex to the Rotunda and reduced both to ruins.

In its day, the Annex fulfilled a purpose. The Public Hall accommodated 1,200 people, who sat on hardwood benches and faced a rostrum, behind which hung from 1857 on a copy of Raphael's *School of Athens*. Executed by the French painter Paul Balze (who had already copied the Renaissance masterpiece for two other clients), the painting was lost in the fire, despite efforts to rescue it by tearing it down. Another copy, incorporated into Stanford White's design for a new auditorium, was installed in Cabell Hall in 1902.

Health and Temperance

Throughout the 1850s, living conditions were not particularly sanitary or healthful. By 1858, according to a map of that time, a circular gymnasium stood south of the Lawn, presumably housing also the Russian steam bath, which students applauded as "a most useful and agreeable substitute for

our present way of bathing—viz.: with a bucket of cold water and a torn towel." Typhoid fever swept through the community in 1856 and 1857, killing five students. The university fumigated the West Range, where disease seemed most prevalent. Month after month during 1858 more students died—six by March. To try to stop the "increase of disease," the visitors suspended classes for six weeks. They also banned hogs on the university grounds (for a second time) and established an infirmary in the building now called Varsity Hall.

Teetotaling professors exhorted students toward abstinence. Their ardor inspired the Sons of Temperance to build a meetinghouse outside the East Range. After the Civil War, the temperance movement waned, and the Temperance Hall became a bookstore, post office, and railroad ticket office. Writing in 1920, the university historian Philip Bruce called this configuration of businesses "the Corner," across the street from the area given that name today.

Next, Godliness

Even before it opened, Jefferson's university suffered a reputation as an institution scornful of religion. Manifestations of tolerance—no classes or professorship in divinity, no affiliation with any denomination—struck some as sacrilegious. In 1829 an Episcopal bishop, preaching a memorial sermon for six

William H. McGuffey, professor of moral philosophy. *McGuffey's "Eclectic Readers" were already well known by the time their author joined the University of Virginia faculty. Trained as a classicist and devoutly Presbyterian, McGuffey taught at the university from 1845 until his death in 1873. His 1855 course description has been cited as the first reference to Shakespeare in any American college catalogue.*

students dead of typhoid, implied that the disease was God's punishment for Jefferson's "disguised Atheism." In 1840 a student wrote a friend that he lived among "a most godless set, professors and students."

In fact, students had practiced religion from the beginning, meeting for devotions in the east wing of the Rotunda. From 1832 on, a university chaplaincy rotated annually among preachers of Virginia's four major faiths, Baptist, Episcopal, Methodist, and Presbyterian. Certain faculty (notably, law professor John B. Minor and professor of moral philosophy William H. McGuffey) exerted a strong moral influence on the students, doing more to shape the university's religious profile than did any of the short-term chaplains. In 1848 McGuffey reported that "over thirty young gentlemen voluntarily" attended morning prayers. Since the Rotunda wing where they worshiped also housed classes in mathematics and anatomy, pious students sought a more sacred space.

In 1858 the university became home to the first college chapter of the Young Men's Christian Association. (Harvard and Princeton Universities supported religious clubs, and a University of Michigan club eventually associated with the YMCA; however, Virginia's chapter was the first attached to the World Alliance, which started in 1855.) The YMCA "succeeded beyond the most sanguine expectations of its friends," read the March 1859 *Virginia University Magazine.* Members joined in mission projects, teaching Bible classes to slaves and mountain folk. One tally reported that the number of "professors of religion" among students doubled in four years, from 97 (out of 558) in 1855 to 200 (out of 606) in 1859.

Pavilion VIII living room. *Pavilion VIII was the home of the earliest mathematics professors, including Charles Bonnycastle, whose portrait here hangs above the mantle.*

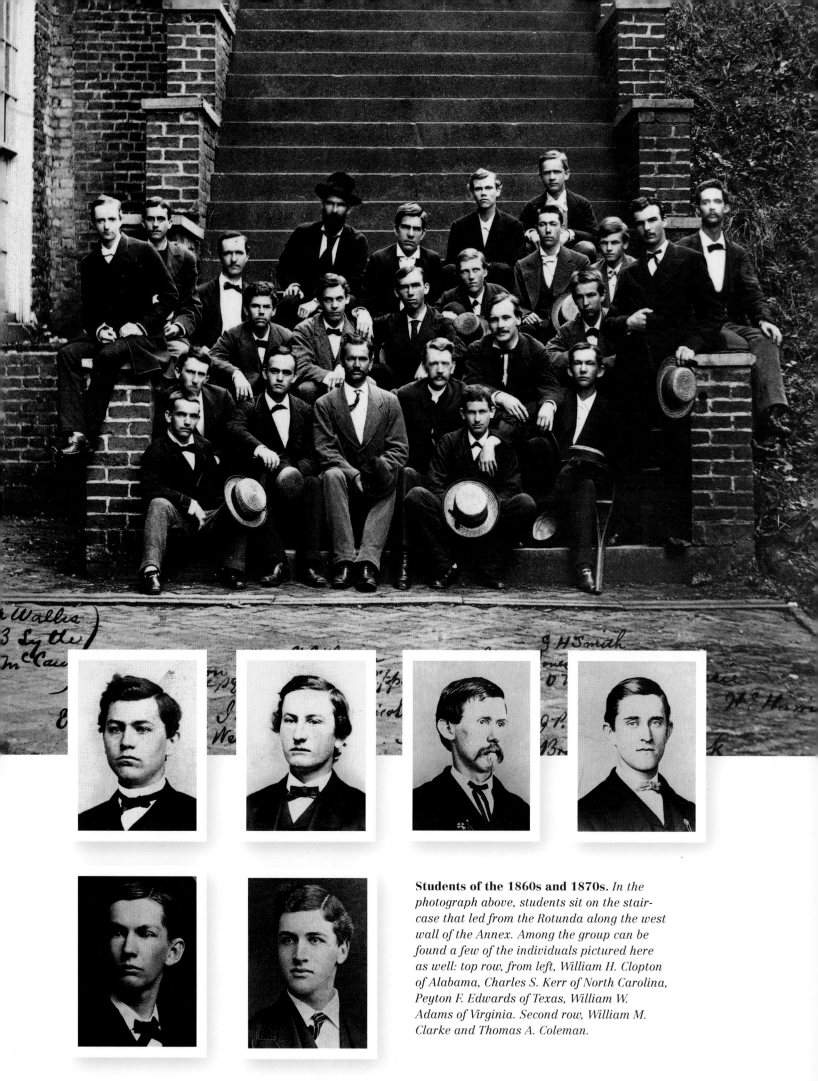

Students of the 1860s and 1870s. *In the photograph above, students sit on the staircase that led from the Rotunda along the west wall of the Annex. Among the group can be found a few of the individuals pictured here as well: top row, from left, William H. Clopton of Alabama, Charles S. Kerr of North Carolina, Peyton F. Edwards of Texas, William W. Adams of Virginia. Second row, William M. Clarke and Thomas A. Coleman.*

Many of "the old boys" of thirty years ago remember the splendid spectacle afforded on commencement evenings when the Rotunda and the Public Hall were a blaze of light, and it seemed impossible that any avenue could be so noble and dazzling as the one from the portico through the Rotunda and the connecting porch into the great hall, where the whole view ended in the rostrum and Raphael's assembled philosophers.

— JOHN S. PATTON, 1906

John Singleton Mosby, soldier and alumnus. *Mosby seems to have been belligerent in his student days. He enrolled in 1850; in 1851 he was fined ten dollars for hitting a constable over the head with a gunstock. Two years later, for shooting a fellow student, Mosby spent seven months in jail, where he began to read the law. He went on to lead Mosby's Raiders, a Confederate band whose attacks on Union bases seriously disabled the Army of the Potomac in the early years of the War between the States.*

War Approaches

At the 1861 celebration of Thomas Jefferson's birthday, the Sons of Liberty (wearing red shirts trimmed with black velvet and brass buttons) and the Southern Guard (wearing blue shirts and light blue caps) marched to rhythmic commands. "The military spirit has become irrepressible," reported the *Virginia University Magazine.* A student at the university, Robert E. Lee Jr., enlisted in the Southern Guard, but his father preferred that he concentrate on studies. As the Southern Guard concluded a drill one morning on the Lawn, a dispatch arrived. "Fort Sumpter has surrendered," their captain read aloud, "and the Palmetto flag now floats over its walls." At that, Captain Hutter later wrote, "a mighty sound went up from the multitude," and "each and every one began to prepare for war."

Rebel colors had already been flown at the university. In February 1861 a small group of students hired a Charlottesville seamstress to sew a Confederate flag out of cheap cambric, then paid a black carpenter, Isaac Sampson, to hew a flagstaff. The students broke into the Rotunda after midnight, "then out to the lightning-rod," wrote one of them, Dr. R. Channing Moore Page, years later. "The wind was high and it was now bitter cold. Dangerous work climbing over that dome by a slender lightning-rod! But we did it.... The flag was given full swing and went to the breeze in splendid style."

Once Virginia seceded from the Union, student brigades mustered. "Things began to hum with excitement," according to Frank S. Robertson, a sergeant of the Sons of Liberty. Student troops joined contingents from Charlottesville and Staunton. Carrying muskets but no ammunition, they boarded boxcars headed for Harper's Ferry, the southernmost Union stronghold. After "a hard but bloodless campaign of ten days, and without the gratification of firing even a blank cartridge from our much admired new arms," alumnus W. Gordon McCabe remembered later, students returned to the university under orders from Virginia's governor.

Faculty formed their own military brigade, "an awkward squad indeed," one called it. "Armed with old-fashioned flint-lock muskets of antiquated pattern, ... which they held at all inclinations to the vertical, they presented the most wonderful variety of movements for each word of command," wrote Professor Francis H. Smith. "Fortunately for the Confederacy," added Smith, "this squad ... was never called to the field.

Mathematics professor Albert T. Bledsoe, a West Point classmate of Jefferson Davis's, was appointed war bureau chief for the Confederacy. Davis appointed Francis Smith to the Confederate Committee of Weights and Measures. Chemistry professor Socrates Maupin advised Confederate troops on artillery and explosives. Basil L. Gildersleeve, professor of Greek, went to war and came back wounded.

Medical faculty James L. Cabell and John Staige Davis stayed on university grounds and tended ailing soldiers. Wounded soldiers arrived in such numbers that tents were erected for them on the Lawn. Henry Martin, the university's bell ringer, recalled in 1914 that hundreds of wounded soldiers were stretched out for treatment in the Rotunda. "It didn't make no difference how much they was sufferin'; they didn't make no noise," he recalled in memories transcribed for the 1914 student yearbook *Corks and Curls.* "No, sir, they lay right still a-lookin' straight up at the ceilin'."

Henry Martin, janitor and bell ringer. *For more than fifty years, students awoke to the sound of Henry Martin's ringing of the bell above the Rotunda's south portico. In 1914, one year before he died, "Uncle Henry" told his life story to the English professor C. Alphonso Smith, who printed it in* Corks and Curls. *Born on 4 July 1826, the day Thomas Jefferson died, Martin was connected with the university from the age of nineteen on. Of his bell ringing, he said, "I been as true to that bell as to my God."*

Basil L. Gildersleeve, professor of ancient languages. *Gildersleeve taught Latin and Greek from 1856 to 1876 and introduced an alphabetical cataloguing system in the university library. He took a leave of absence to fight for the Confederacy and sustained wounds that left him crippled for life.*

Confederate veterans. *Many University of Virginia students and alumni joined Confederate forces during the War between the States. After the war, 117 veteran alumni survived. Eighty of those men, including those pictured above, returned to the university in 1912 to be honored for their war efforts.*

Union Troops in Charlottesville

General Sheridan's troops were moving through Virginia, having defeated General Jubal Early on 2 March 1865 near Waynesboro. The university community had reason to fear his approach, remembering how Union troops had burned down barracks at Virginia Military Institute the summer before.

Classes continued, but "with wandering thoughts on the part of both teacher and pupils," Professor John Minor noted. Sixty years later, Judge R. T. W. Duke Jr. recalled that "the news *froze* our *blood.* Was it—could it be—possible that these *awful creatures* were to come to us. We had heard of Sheridan—of his *ruthless plundering—burning* of *dwelling houses* and all the fiendish acts which characterized his raids in the Valley of Virginia. We dreaded his approach." Duke remembered watching, to the sound of martial music from afar, a "long semingly [*sic*] endless column move along like a great blue snake" toward the university.

A delegation met General George Armstrong Custer, head of the invading troops. Socrates Maupin, chairman of the faculty, John B. Minor, professor of law, and Colonel Thomas L. Preston, university rector, joined city elders at the tollgate (near today's northeast corner of Alderman Library), waving the flag of truce. "We announced to these men," Minor wrote in his diary, "that no defense of Charlottesville was contemplated, that the town was evacuated, and that we requested protection for the University, and for the town." Minor got no sleep the next two nights. On Sunday, 5 March, General William T. Sherman searched the university. "They were as civil as

possible and of course found nothing contraband," Minor recorded. After four days the Union troops moved on toward Petersburg. They spared the university but left a swath of destruction behind.

War's Aftermath

Almost all amenities disappeared at the university from 1861 to 1865. No meetings of the literary societies or the YMCA were held; neither the magazine nor the catalogue was published. In 1862 the university enrolled only forty-six students, but the faculty and visitors were determined to keep the university open.

As soon as war ended, students returned: 258 in 1865; 490 in 1866, more from outside Virginia than from the Commonwealth. The University of Virginia regained enrollment more quickly than did other southern universities during Reconstruction, faring equally well as the nation slid into an economic depression during the 1870s. Private donations to the school during its first forty years had totaled about sixty thousand dollars, but they reached ten times that in the twenty-five years after the war.

Industrialization and urbanization affected the culture of the University of Virginia in these postwar decades. Students came in greater numbers from professional and mercantile families in Virginia's growing urban centers. One historian estimates that while cities represented only a tenth of the Commonwealth's population, nearly a third of Virginia residents at the university in the academic year 1881–82 came from Richmond, Norfolk, Alexandria, Lynchburg, Portsmouth, or Petersburg.

Socrates Maupin, professor of chemistry and pharmacy. *From its founding through the nineteenth century, the university had no president. The Board of Visitors made financial decisions, and the faculty made administrative decisions. Socrates Maupin, who taught chemistry in both the academic and the medical divisions, was named chair of the faculty one year after coming to the university. He held that post from 1854 until 1870 and was among those who met Union troops as they approached the university grounds.*

73

The faculty, 1866. *Just after the Civil War, the university faculty—shown here in a composite portrait created for Bohn's Album—numbered fourteen. In the outer circle, from top right clockwise: Basil L. Gildersleeve, Charles S. Venable, Socrates Maupin, Stephen O. Southall, John Staige Davis, S. F. Chancellor, John B. Minor, Maximilian Schele de Vere, William E. Peters, Francis H. Smith. In the inner circle, from top clockwise: George F. Holmes, Henry Howard, William H. McGuffey, James L. Cabell.*

Graduate and professional programs solidified in the 1880s. The university established the modern degree sequence, up through the doctor of philosophy degree, first granted in 1880. Students could attain an "academic" degree, bachelor's or master's; the more general designation of "proficiency" or "graduate"; or a professional degree in law, medicine, or engineering.

Law offerings were divided between common and statute law on the one hand and constitutional and international law on the other. For a degree in law, one studied both. Using colorful language (probably written by Professor Minor), the faculty urged—but did not require—two years of study: "One cannot expect to gorge himself with law, as a boa-constrictor does with masses of food, and then digest it afterwards; the process of assimilation must go on, if it is to proceed healthfully and beneficially, at the same time with the reception of knowledge."

The degree of doctor of medicine was first granted in 1868. By 1890 medical students studied basic life sciences, using newly acquired microscopes, followed by a year of clinical study in the dispensary and hospital. Classes were small, allowing students to examine patients as part of their training. Dissections took place in the Anatomical Theater, and medical students heard "didactic lectures" in descriptive, surgical, and topographical anatomy, complementing the practical anatomy they learned through work on cadavers.

Engineering coalesced into a department in 1881, with faculty from mathematics and the sciences emphasizing the practical problems of mines, machines, bridges, roads, railroads, and power. By the 1890s engineering shops in the Rotunda Annex were humming as faculty, students, and technical staff operated a twenty-five-horsepower steam engine, a steam boiler, an Edison dynamo, and machining tools.

In 1878 Leander J. McCormick, who with his older brother, Cyrus, had amassed a fortune in harvesting machines, gave the university a thirty-two-foot telescope with a twenty-six-inch lens, the largest in the United States at the time. "Think of a University," an editor of the student magazine

Medical students, 1873. *Students studying medicine at the university stand here before the Anatomical Theater, which held classes in anatomy and surgery until 1938, when it was torn down to make way for the construction of Alderman Library.*

Walter Reed, medical investigator and alumnus. *Among the first to receive a degree in medicine from the University of Virginia, Reed completed his year of medical course work in 1869, at the age of eighteen. He joined the army medical corps in 1875 and in 1900 began the investigations in Cuba that led to the discovery of the cause of yellow fever.*

William Mynn Thornton, first dean of engineering. *Thornton taught Greek at Davidson College in North Carolina before joining the University of Virginia faculty as a professor of applied mathematics in 1875. He taught at the university for fifty years, building and diversifying its offerings in the various fields of engineering.*

had complained in 1860, "utterly destitute of an astronomical observatory." By 1886 the university was advertising courses for "practical astronomers." At McCormick Observatory students and faculty began building the university's collection of parallax images, timed photographs of stars and planets, useful as late as the 1960s in that they represented more than fifty years' worth of sky images, essential in calculating the distance of stars from the earth.

With more students and more buildings, the task of running the university was becoming more complex. Many of those who labored for the university have been lost in history, but their contributions are epitomized in the person of Martin Tracy, who worked through much of the nineteenth century as the university's janitor. Once the university had recovered after the war years, Tracy successfully petitioned the Board of Visitors for a raise in pay, enumerating the many services he performed:

I have to be up every morning before five o'clock a.m. to give out ice, and close the icehouse at six a.m.... I have to help Dr. Maupin his lecture days, and if any of his chemical apparatus is out of order or broken, I have to mend it.... I have to keep the big clock in order, and the clock in the chapel, and also one in Dr. Maupin's lecture-room. Also, I have to sharpen Dr. Cabell's surgical instruments and also Dr. Davis's. Also I have to be the plumber in stopping leaks in the pipes, or the hydrants.... I put up, last winter, a new force pump in place of the old one that was broken by frost.... I have to drive the engine once or twice a week to keep a supply of water in the tanks. And I have to mend all the locks and keys for each room. I have to show visitors through the public rooms, and have to help to put in glass in the windows and to help Mr. Wertenbaker to fix the diplomas.

Astronomical equipment. *A gift from Leander J. McCormick, the brother and business partner of Cyrus McCormick, allowed the university to build an astronomical observatory, fulfilling a plan that Jefferson had envisioned. Equipment allowed observation and the creation of photographic records of stellar and planetary movement.*

The Burgeoning 1890s

In 1876 the New York textile magnate Lewis Brooks, identified publicly only as a "Northern friend of Southern Education," gave money for a museum and "a cabinet of Natural Science." The university constructed an ornate three-story building to house thousands of specimens—bones, fossils, minerals, plant samples—laid out in evolutionary sequence. "Here is a full procession of life through the ages," wrote a scientific journal in 1878. Plaster replicas of a South American glyptodon (a dinosaur) and a Siberian mammoth dominated the two-story display room until, to make room for renovations, the outmoded beasts were reduced to rubble in 1948.

Contemporaries heralded the building, but twentieth-century critics have not. A 1913 *Corks and Curls* article called it "an anachronism produc-

The Natural History Museum.
Brooks Hall, completed in 1877 and pictured here around 1890, was built to house a "cabinet of Natural Science," with artifacts arrayed so as to evoke the sequence of natural evolution. Around the building's perimeter, gargoyles (inset) gaze out from beneath the names of great life scientists.

78

ing a discord." Although renovated in 1948 for more useful offices and classrooms, Brooks Hall faced demolition in 1977. The restored Rotunda had just opened, and the neo-Gothic building at its northeast corner seemed a disrespectful eyesore. Community advocates rallied, however, and Brooks Hall was saved.

The mission to build a chapel resurfaced. To raise funds, a Ladies Chapel Aid Society staged a "Mikado Tea," lit by Japanese lanterns, and a "Mother Goose Entertainment," with hostesses dressed as nursery-rhyme characters. In 1885 the university laid the cornerstone for a neo-Gothic chapel, symbolizing "the contrast between earthly wisdom and heavenly truth," with the Rotunda portraying a pagan temple's "cold though classic beauty" and the chapel "aspiring to heaven," proclaimed Professor Maximilian

Inside Brooks Hall. *The museum's collection included gems, fossils, plant specimens, and—in the middle of the display hall—these massive plaster models of a glyptodon dinosaur skeleton and a Siberian mammoth.*

Schele de Vere. Delays arose over the stained-glass windows, some of which arrived broken. In 1890 the chapel opened for worship.

Students still clamored for athletics. One student, Edward H. Squibb, so passionately wanted exercise facilities that in 1876 he bought equipment and, allied with more than one hundred students, forced the university to find a place for it. Hotel F became a gymnasium, with parallel bars, rings, a trapeze, rowing machines, punching bags, and weights for lifting. By 1890 every student underwent a physical exam and received a personalized "hand-book of developing exercise."

By the 1890s Virginia had football and baseball teams engaged in intercollegiate competition. The school anthem emerged amid enthusiasm over the winning football team of 1893. As students awaited the team at the C & O railroad station, they transformed familiar ballads into pep songs, and "Auld Lang Syne" became "The Good Old Song." "It sprang spontaneously from hundreds of glowing hearts," wrote alumnus Edward A. Craighill Jr., responsible for recording the first verse and composing others, including this second verse, specific to the occasion of the song's origin:

> *We come from old Virginia,*
> *Where all is mirth and glee;*
> *Let's all join hands and give a yell*
> *For the team of ninety-three.*

Exercise moved in 1893 into Fayerweather Hall, the largest and best-equipped physical education facility in the South. An indoor swimming pool measured twenty-five by forty feet, filled with sixty thousand gallons of unheated water. The building housed bowling alleys, a ball cage, an exercise room, a locker room, and a cantilevered track. In the basement were "baths of every variety—tubs, shower, needle, douche and sponge baths," with hot water "for legitimate use, but not in superabundance."

Rowing crew, one of the university's first intercollegiate teams. *In 1859 students established a cricket club at the university; but war soon interrupted its games, and it never reappeared. In 1876 the Rives Boat Club was formed, supported financially by New York alumnus Francis H. Rives. Here, the crew of 1882, including coxswain John P. Nelson (right).*

During the 1890s, new degree programs were established, new student and alumnus activities proliferated—including the daily student newspaper, the student yearbook, and the alumni magazine—and athletics became an everyday part of student life, as students joined on-grounds teams and cheered for their new intercollegiate teams as well. These photographs, taken from student scrapbooks, give a sense of the times. Notice in the bottom photo a copy of College Topics, *the new student newspaper, hanging behind the young man's head.*

Familiar scenes. *Details of style may differ, but these University of Virginia students of the 1890s, relaxing in chairs drawn out into the sunshine or posing for a camera on the Lawn, look remarkably similar to students a century later.*

The Great Fire

After struggling through a war and hard times, by 1895 the University of Virginia had regained its stride. Football and baseball teams now played in intercollegiate competition. Eighteen fraternities had opened chapters, although none had yet opened a residence. *College Topics,* the student daily, started in 1890; *Corks and Curls,* the student yearbook, in 1893. In 1894 the Society of Alumni started publishing its *Alumni Bulletin.* The university was bustling with new buildings, new activities, and new accomplishments. Few remembered Thomas Jefferson Randolph's warning that the Annex might cause destruction.

It was a Sunday morning, 27 October 1895. At ten o'clock, many were attending church services. Mason Foshee, a student from Alabama, noticed smoke escaping the northwest corner of the Annex roof. He alerted janitor Henry Martin, who set to ringing the Rotunda bell. Staff, students, and faculty and their wives scrambled to fight the fire and rescue what contents they could,

Corks and Curls. *In 1888 students established a yearbook, named Corks and Curls—slang for failures and successes. Students with no answers sat mouths shut like corked bottles; students with answers, receiving praise, looked like dogs curling their tails in delight. Those, at least, were the etymologies offered in an essay submitted by a medical student named Leander Fogg. University rolls show no one with that name; likely it was a playful pseudonym created by the editors.*

The fire of 1895. *By midday on Sunday, 27 October 1895, most of Charlottesville had congregated to watch the conflagration that all but leveled Jefferson's Rotunda and the Annex. Faculty and students undertook heroic efforts to rescue books and furniture, separate the Annex from the Rotunda, and soak nearby buildings on the Lawn, all to keep the fire from spreading.*

ultimately watching with horror as flames devoured the Annex and Rotunda in two hours' time.

Students ran into the buildings, salvaging furniture and equipment. They threw books out windows; ladies below held their skirts up to catch them. They wrestled the white marble sculpture of Jefferson, estimated to weigh two thousand pounds, out onto the Lawn.

"There was no water," explained the 1896 *Corks and Curls.* "The pressure in the mains, though originally adequate, had been reduced by the roughening and rusting of the pipes till the stream was too feeble to be effectual. There was no fire engine, the only one which the University had ever possessed having long since rusted out in 'innocuous desuetude.' Telegrams were sent to all adjacent towns for aid; but even while sending the dispatches we knew that aid must come too late."

Fire's aftermath. *By Sunday afternoon the fire had been extinguished, and a smoldering Rotunda stood open to the sky. Annex pillars stood alongside like ancient ruins, the roof they had held, demolished.*

"It was an awful scene," wrote Morgan Poitiaux Robinson ten years later. "The smoke was so thick and dense that one could not see twenty feet from him; the jingle of glass which was being knocked and kicked out of the book-cases; dozens of men and boys all shouting different things; the crashing of beams accompanying the frequent explosions of dynamite cartridges; the roar of the flames which were now well in the room and cast a dull, red, fiendish glow over everything through the smoke; the crackling of burning timbers; all these things tended to make a veritable hell."

William H. Echols, professor of mathematics. *Echols, one of many faculty to fight the great fire, scaled the Rotunda roof in his efforts to save the building. He was a memorable figure who taught at the university from 1891 to 1934. After his death a plaque was mounted on Pavilion VIII, where he lived, commemorating his "ruthless insistence that the supreme values are self respect, integrity of mind, contempt of fear and hatred of sham."*

"Blow down the Portico! was the cry," an alumnus reported. Mathematics professor William H. Echols believed that he might save the Rotunda by eliminating the breezeway between the two buildings. Thirty-six-year-old Echols carried fifty pounds of dynamite up onto the dome of the Rotunda and flung it down on the breezeway roof. "Suddenly there was a fearful explosion as though the heavens had been rent asunder," recalled Robinson. "The next moment all was silence; we were in total darkness; the whole earth seemed to tremble; the Rotunda rocked; the voices hushed."

"The whole dome seemed to shiver," remembered another eyewitness, Anna Barringer, who lived on the Lawn at the time. "The hundreds of spectators gave that a-a-ah of irrevocable loss—someone shouted, 'There she goes,' and the dome dropped solidly into the holocaust below. Tears were unabashed on my face, because something beautiful that I had loved had ended helpless in distress and could never be again."

Needless to say, Echols's strategy had not worked. Instead, a draft sucked flames into the Rotunda. "It was a magnificent sight to look on that

The day after the fire, Bell Dunnington, daughter of Professor Francis Dunnington, wrote the following letter to her sister.

Oct. 28, 1895

My Dear Sadie

By the time you get this letter you will have heard of the dreadful fire we have had here; and how the dear old Rotunda is all burned down, and nothing left standing but the walls, the front and back porches, and some blackened pillars.... I never saw a more magnificent or more awful sight than when the dome caught fire. All of the top part of it was one terrible, glowing mass of flame, and the tin had a curious reddish look, though it did not blaze, but wrinkled up. Every student in the University must have been there and I never saw anybody work as they did.... Mr. Echols hurt his arm, and one or two students fainted from heat and fatigue. The old clock stopped at five minutes to twelve, and not very long after all the wood around it was burnt away, and it fell, with a crash, down on the pavement.... Two long lines of men were formed down East Lawn and branches going down each alley to the hydrants. In one line the buckets were going up to the Rotunda and on the other coming down again.... Last night it looked as if the whole Rotunda was lit up from top to bottom....

Your affectionate sister
Bell Dunnington

gigantic roaring furnace as the fresh air rushed in and cleared away the smoke," wrote Robinson. "Here the pedestal of the marble statue, ... there some dusty books left to their fate on the shelves in the library; here a broken bookcase on the floor; and there a perfect volcano of flame pouring into the Rotunda from the Annex, and in a minute a cloud of smoke shutting off everything in view." Nearby student rooms and pavilions had been water-soaked to keep the fire from spreading. When the wind shifted from north to south, blowing the flames back toward the Annex, firefighters knew "the danger of further destruction was over."

Investigation over the next three days revealed that the fire was probably caused by electrical wiring strung above the ceiling into the Public Hall. Although the dynamo that generated power for all the university's lighting was, as usual, not operating on Sunday morning, the dynamo powering the electric trolley line from Charlottesville did start up at 8:20. Electric lights had flared or burst at several locations near the university grounds in the hour before the fire began. "It is doubtful whether the origin will ever be securely established," investigators recorded in the faculty minutes on 31 October 1895, but they suspected that a surge of power had jumped from the trolley to the lighting lines, which ran parallel to one another.

The Rotunda was a charred shell. Three walls and detached portico columns were all that remained of the Annex. Books strewn across the Lawn were later collected and stacked inside the natural history museum for safekeeping. Of the library's fifty thousand volumes, seventeen thousand were saved.

Monday, the day after the fire, all classes met, although many in new locations. The University of Virginia embarked on its second reconstruction in thirty years.

The Annex after the fire. *Three Annex walls remained standing, even though the source of the fire was traced back to faulty electrical wiring running above the ceiling of the Annex's Public Hall.*

THE GREEKS

The first fraternities at the University of Virginia were social clubs, not residences—and secret clubs at that. In 1852 six young men met privately and secured a charter from Delta Kappa Epsilon, whose parent organization was located at Yale. In 1853 DKE members would disclose neither club rules nor proposed activities in their request for official recognition, which was refused by a skeptical faculty. Members met anyway, in private and after dark, keeping their meeting places and their memberships confidential.

In 1859 fifteen such "secret societies" existed at the university, according to the *Virginia University Magazine*. Ten were the predecessors of fraternities still in existence: Delta Kappa Epsilon, Chi Phi, Sigma Alpha Epsilon, Beta Theta Pi, Zeta Psi, Sigma Chi, Alpha Tau Omega, Chi Psi, and Pi Kappa Alpha. The magazine also reported the existence of the "Mystic Seven," precursor to today's still mysterious Seven Society, and the Sons of Confucius, numbering only four members. The size of secret societies ranged from four to sixteen members, but all told more than 150 students belonged, about one-quarter of the student body.

Social clubs suspended activities during the War of Secession but soon regained vigor. In the late 1860s all but one member of the university's DKE chapter had been a soldier or officer during the war. Two national fraternities were founded during that era in student rooms at the University of Virginia: Pi Kappa Alpha, in 1868, in 31 West Range; and Kappa Sigma, in 1869, in 46 East Lawn. Kappa Sigma located its national headquarters in Charlottesville.

By the turn of the century, almost half of all university students belonged to fraternities. Starting in the 1880s, fraternities built residences for their members. DKE opened a cottage on Carr's Hill, although it was deeded to the university in case the fraternity defaulted. From there, DKE brothers moved into a house on Fourteenth Street, the first independently owned fraternity residence.

Jefferson Society members lived together in Blue Cottage on Carr's Hill, 1867. Above: pins and ribbon belonging to Kappa Sigma founder William McCormick.

In 1915 the university's first Jewish fraternity, Zeta Beta Tau, opened with six members. When ZBT vacated its Emmet Street house across from Memorial Gymnasium in 1936, the university's alumni association acquired and moved into that building, which, renovated and expanded, has served as alumni headquarters ever since.

By the 1920s fraternities dominated the neighborhood north of the Rotunda, with Rugby Road to the west and Chancellor Street to the east. New houses, often designed with imposing neoclassic lines, accommodated growing memberships, offering dining and social areas as well as student rooms. First Delta Psi constructed a residence at 133 Chancellor Street. It took the name of St. Anthony Hall, after the fraternity's patron saint, who, according to a 1947 booklet on fraternities at Virginia, was "subject to virtually endless temptations by Satan, the

Above: Fraternity party, ca. 1970. Right: IMPs cross Beta Bridge, ca. 1983. Below: Zeta Beta Tau with dates and house mothers, ca. 1920.

Above: Phi Beta Sigma pledges, ca. 1980. Right: Madison Lane, seen from Phi Psi window.

bulk of which appear to have taken the form of mass attack by liberal minded females." Other residences of note to follow include that of Zeta Psi, built on Rugby Road in 1926 and designed by architecture instructor Louis F. Voorhees, and that of Sigma Nu, also built in 1926, on Carr's Hill, and designed by the Washington, D.C., architect Louis Justement.

From the 1920s through the 1960s, Greek-letter culture dominated student life. *Corks and Curls,* the yearbook, was published by the fraternities. Those who held positions of power in the university—editors of the newspaper and magazines, officers of the student council—almost always belonged to fraternities. Membership by "rush" meant that certain types of student tended to congregate in particular houses, and one's fraternity affiliation came to carry implications about one's character—as displayed in a prank set of fraternity applications published in the November 1954 issue of *Spectator* magazine. The Alpha Epsilon Pi application posed a difficult mathematical problem. The Chi Phi application asked for a list of country-club memberships. The SAE application asked for a gridiron number. The St. Anthony Hall application asked for family history: "During which period did your family settle in Virginia, 1607–1700, 1700–1750, or 1750–1800?"

Through the middle decades of the twentieth century, fraternities dominated students' social life

at Virginia as well. On party weekends like Midwinters and Easters, the university sponsored one or two main events, but fraternities hosted ball games, teas, cocktail hours, and late-night parties, filling in the schedule with activities from ten in the morning to the wee hours of the night. Each spring the Easters issue of the student newspaper printed the names of hundreds of female visitors, listed by hosting fraternities.

A few sororities opened university chapters early on. In 1924, four years after women were admitted to graduate study, a local sorority began: Pi Chi. In 1932 Pi Chi affiliated with Kappa Delta, joining Chi Omega to become the first national sororities at Virginia. A third sorority, Zeta Tau Alpha, installed a University of Virginia chapter in 1952. None drew a large enough membership to warrant a residence, but Mary Munford Hall, opened in 1951, included chapter rooms where sororities could hold meetings. "At times sorority membership here has been low—down to one or two women in each

Instead of "rushing" prospective members, some of these fraternities required rituals of self-control, such as walking in line, carrying symbolic paddles, or standing at attention in public without speaking. "It's meant to be impossible," an Alpha Phi Alpha fraternity member, Timothy Smith, explained to a *Daily Progress* reporter in 1977. "One's mettle is tested." Such rituals were the most visible evidence of black fraternal organizations on the university grounds, but the primary dedication of their membership was in the broader community, through charitable service projects.

Kappa Delta sisters, ca. 1940. Right: Chuck Berry at Memorial Gymnasium, 1965.

sorority," read a 1960 article in the *Charlottesville Daily Progress*, "but these one or two members have always been able to keep the Greek organizations alive." Once full undergraduate coeducation was adopted at the university, the number of sororities at Virginia increased swiftly.

In the 1970s traditionally black fraternities and sororities established chapters, bringing a different Greek-letter tradition to the University of Virginia.

Celebrating a Century

Edwin Anderson Alderman, first president of the university

Four days after fire destroyed the Rotunda, faculty conveyed their proposals for rebuilding. The Rotunda should be reconstructed with fireproof materials, they believed, its original proportions "religiously observed." The Annex, "an architectural blunder," should not be reconstructed but should be replaced by four buildings placed elsewhere on the grounds: an academical building, including a horseshoe-shaped public hall; a laboratory for "delicate physical experimentation"; an engineering building, isolated from others since it would house "coal-sheds, boiler-house, engine-room, and so on"; and a law building. All these buildings, the faculty urged, should be designed "so as to create an harmonious combination with the original Jeffersonian group." Four months later, the architect Stanford White presented drawings for a new Rotunda and three new buildings facing it at the opposite end of the Lawn.

In 1896, New York–based McKim, Mead & White was the nation's premier architectural firm, known for the Boston Public Library and campus buildings at Columbia and New York Universities. Stanford White became the liaison with the university, living in Albemarle County while the work went on. He submitted two ideas for rebuilding the Rotunda, but he favored the one that reinterpreted

1920

- **1,600 students**

- **140 faculty members**

- **College tuition and fees: $10 for Virginians; $175 for non-Virginians**

- **Lawn rooms: $75 per year; Range rooms: $72 per year**

- **At the University Shop at the Corner, shoes cost $7, suits cost $35, and shirts cost $1.50**

- **At the Jefferson Theater downtown, tickets cost 35¢ to $2**

Rotunda scaffolding. *Reconstruction of the Rotunda took five years, from 1895 to 1900. Meanwhile, university life went on.*

Democracy: A Pageant. *In 1918 the university staged this pageant (left), composed by Anna Barringer, daughter of medical professor Paul B. Barringer.*

John W. Mallet, professor of industrial and applied chemistry. *Mallet (far left) was considered kind to students while tolerating no familiarity. He criticized the liberty given to Stanford White in redesigning the Rotunda.*

Rector Wilson Cary Nicholas Randolph. *Randolph (left), a great-grandson of Thomas Jefferson's, served as rector from 1890 to 1897, overseeing the plans to rebuild the Rotunda after the fire.*

Room to expand. *Jefferson envisioned the university's extending the colonnades and adding more dormitories and pavilions to accommodate its growing population. Topography did not allow such expansion, however, and in 1896 the university rector agreed to Stanford White's suggestion to build at the south end of the Lawn.*

its interior space, removing the third-level floor and creating the two-story Dome Room.

The news of the firm's plans to redesign Jefferson's Rotunda threw the university into an uproar. John W. Mallet, professor of chemistry, blamed William Thornton, since the faculty report, penned by Thornton, had allowed the architect to "design the interior of the building that the whole of the capacity from the dome down to the portico floor may hereafter be readily and simply utilizable for Library purposes." The Board of Visitors—led by the rector Wilson Cary Nicholas Randolph, Thomas Jefferson's great-grandson—selected White's preferred design. Construction began in June 1896.

White also designed three new buildings to make up for the Annex's lost teaching space. Privately, he expressed more doubt about this variation on Jefferson's vision than about that on the Rotunda. "I'm scared to

Until the fire, few people knew the university or Jefferson's brilliance as its architect, because it was remote from the centers of art and culture in nineteenth-century America. . . . The fire set in motion a series of events that attracted gifts, support, and publicity, enhancing the university's reputation and raising expectations for its role in the twentieth century.

— FREDERICK D. NICHOLS, 1981

To the question of the remodeling of the interior of the Rotunda, we have given most careful study. Reasons of sentiment would point to the restoration of the interior exactly as it stood, but ... it was only practical necessity which forced Jefferson at the time it was built to cut the Rotunda in two stories.... [H]e would have planned the interior as a simple, single and noble room had he then been able to do so.

— McKim, Mead & White, 1896

The new quadrangle. *The New York architectural firm of McKim, Mead & White designed not only the reconstructed Rotunda but also three buildings at the south end of the Lawn: the Physical Laboratory to the west (now Rouss Hall), the Mechanical Laboratory to the east (now Cocke Hall), and a classroom building to the south (now Old Cabell Hall), completed in 1902.*

death. I only hope I can do it right," he told a friend. Again he submitted two ideas. In the one he called the "most practical," the new buildings stood beside the Lawn. In the other, which he called the "most natural and architectural finish," they stood at the Lawn's south end, facing the Rotunda. The visitors chose the latter design, and in 1898 the university inaugurated three new buildings: Cabell Hall, dedicated to the arts and letters; Rouss Hall, housing the physical sciences; and the Mechanical Laboratory, later named Cocke Hall. Jefferson's Lawn, which once looked out to the Blue Ridge, became a closed quadrangle.

Stanford White, architect. *White's New York firm, McKim, Mead & White, was considered one of the nation's finest when it was hired by the university's Board of Visitors to design a reconstructed Rotunda.*

The University's First President

The problems the university faced at the turn of the century—rebuilding the Rotunda, constructing major buildings, and running a more complex university—raised the issue of the need for a president. Jefferson had intended the university to operate without one. The rector and Board of Visitors managed property, personnel, and finances; academic decisions were made by the faculty, led by a chairman selected from among them. In a crisis—finding a law professor in 1826, student riots in 1845, and now rebuilding the Lawn—suggestions of a president resurfaced. As the university entered the twentieth century, it needed someone "with nothing to do but to lead," as Professor Francis H. Smith put it. In 1902 the Board of Visitors offered the position to Woodrow Wilson, a law alumnus of the university, but he declined. In 1904 Edwin Anderson Alderman accepted, becoming the university's first, and to date its longest-serving, president.

As a student I used to see President Alderman from a distance. He was one of the grandest looking people I ever saw. He had a fine head and fine face and was very kind to all of us, but we kept our distance. Not a one of us ever would have thought of opening our peepers about anything that he did or said.

— COLGATE W. DARDEN, 1978

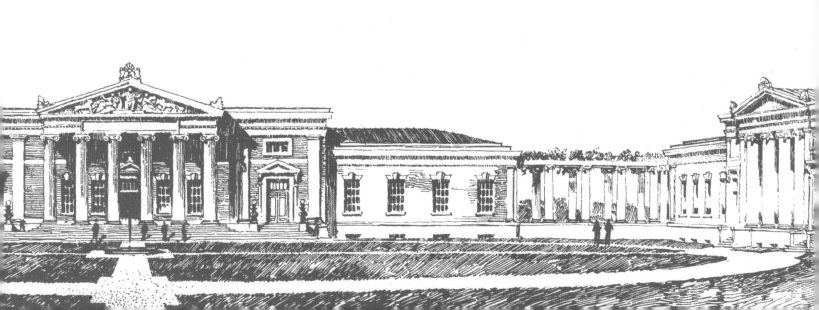

Alderman was a disciple of the educator J. L. M. Curry, who sought to improve public education throughout the South. After running teacher institutes in North Carolina, Alderman had become president of the University of North Carolina, then of Tulane University. Since he was neither a Virginian nor an alumnus of the university, some questioned his appointment. Others saw it, as the *New York Tribune* wrote, as a bold

move that "links the University of Virginia, with all its traditions and its powerful influence on southern thought, with the movement for the democratization of education." Alderman was inaugurated on 13 April 1905, a Founder's Day full of regalia, the first time academic robes were ever worn at the university.

Summer institutes include women. *At the turn of the century, young women participated in summer institutes at the university. Above, women practice principles of nutritious food preparation. Below, summer students gather for a final ceremony.*

The Profession of Education

One of Alderman's primary goals was reached within a year, with the founding of the Curry Memorial School of Education. Faculty in 1880 had already campaigned for a professorship of pedagogy, respecting a growing obligation to the public schools. The faculty even proposed "the admission

to this new department of women who are already teachers, or who may desire to become teachers." Neither proposal won board approval, but change was imminent. Education courses, and later the School of Education itself, led the University of Virginia in considering women and African Americans as part of its faculty and student body.

As early as 1880, the university offered summer classes for teachers. By 1902 a six-week institute hosted teachers, female as well as male, black as well as white, although African American participants, more than sixty among a thousand in 1903, attended class off the grounds. The *Alumni Bulletin* reported that any returning alumnus "would be astonished to find boarding-houses and dormitories filled, and lawns and arcades crowded with earnest-faced men and women. Almost all ages are represented."

T.I.L.K.A. *In the early 1900s, student leaders were usually "ribbon men." They belonged to ribbon societies like T.I.L.K.A. or Eli Banana, which hosted the university's popular germans, or dances. In this photo the 1912 members of T.I.L.K.A. admit their identity.*

The university mace. *One of the many gifts presented by the Seven Society to the university is this silver mace, intricately ornamented with scenes and symbols of the University of Virginia. Carried at the head of every official procession, it was donated on 13 April 1961.*

Social Clubs

In 1905 about seven hundred students attended the university. Fraternities were building and buying houses, clustered in the neighborhood north of the Rotunda. "When will this increase in the number of University fraternities stop?" the student newspaper asked. In 1906 the university agreed to the construction of fraternities on its own property, in the Carr's Hill area. A new circle road, now Culbreth Road, arced around for access to the area.

A lucky few of the hundred-some fraternity men also belonged to Eli Banana, T.I.L.K.A., or Zeta—"ribbon societies," so called because when a member was discovered, he was tagged with a ribbon. Membership "denoted class," university historian Philip Bruce quotes a 1913 student as saying. "The ribbon societies include many leaders in college life, especially those who can scintillate at a pink

The Hot Feet and the IMPs. *Donning robes and devils' horns, members of the Hot Feet Society played pranks on faculty and fellow students until, in 1908, the faculty banned the club, stating that it promoted disorder. Soon thereafter, the IMPs appeared. On 7 April 1920, a thousand people gathered to witness the arrival of B-ski, king of the IMPs. Trumpets announced his arrival in a four-horse barouche. He wore ermine and a jeweled crown—or so College Topics reported—and carried the Hot Feet shield impaled on a trident. That weekend in Fayerweather Gym—with walls shrouded in black and red lights flickering—the new king was crowned. Below, a more homemade version of the crown of the Hot Feet.*

A morning german, 1896. *Dapper students and their well-dressed lady friends sit on the steps of the Rotunda, posing during a "morning german"— a dance, sponsored by one of the student ribbon societies.*

When eight years old [in 1903] I was allowed to watch a morning German, young ladies in picture hats, long full skirts and pompadours or Psyche knot hair arrangements, ... attended by gallant gentlemen with straw hats, blue flannel coats, or striped blazers and white duck trousers. Since there was no Hollywood to sublimate the adolescent imagination, these were the gods and goddesses in our Olympian world who carried an enchanting aura of admiration.

— ANNA BARRINGER,
DAUGHTER OF PROFESSOR
PAUL A. BARRINGER, 1965

University of Virginia
Complimentary German,
Leve Opera House, Charlottesville, Va.
Monday Evening, Oct. 30, 1899.

University of Va. German Club.
Morning German,
Fayerweather Gymnasium,
MONDAY, JUNE 12th, 1899.

FALL GERMAN
OF THE
University of Virginia German Club
FAYERWEATHER GYMNASIUM
FRIDAY EVENING, OCT. 9, 1896

MONDAY GERMAN
OF EASTER WEEK
UNIVERSITY OF VA.
GERMAN CLUB,
FAYERWEATHER GYMNASIUM,
April 3rd, 1899.

WEDNESDAY GERMAN
Easter Week
UNIVERSITY OF VIRGINIA GERMAN CLUB
FAYERWEATHER GYMNASIUM,
April 21st, 1897.

tea or go through a ten course dinner without missing the right fork. No athlete, however great, without a touch of fashion, can get in."

The ultra-secret Seven Society must have begun in this era as well, although evidence only hints at its existence through the twentieth century. At a dance to celebrate the end of World War I, with anonymous invitations issued to both guests and musicians, confetti in the shape of sevens drifted down from the rafters at midnight. In 1947 a check for $17,777.77 to create an emergency fund for students appeared on the bursar's desk. The silver mace carried at the head of university processions and the electronic chimes installed in the chapel in 1957 came through the generosity of the Seven Society. Membership is revealed only on death, when the chapel chimes ring seven times.

The Raven Society, founded in 1904, kept neither members nor motivations secret. Its 1905 album quotes a medical student, William McCully James, who believed that among all the clubs at the university, "there was no single one founded strictly on *merit*." Naming themselves after Edgar Allan Poe's raven, charter members included Armistead M. Dobie, a St. Louis lawyer soon to return to the university as a member of the law faculty, and John Lee Pratt, later a General Motors vice president and a benefactor of the sciences at the university. Through the twentieth century, the Raven Society continued to honor students, faculty, staff, and alumni who performed outstanding service for the university.

Ribbon societies hosted "germans," or dances, often in the morning.

You are requested to appear without accompaniment at No. 13 W·R° on the night of *Thursday, May 3* at *11:35* o'clock in the evening, Rotunda time.

PROMPTNESS   SECRECY

KNOCK THREE TIMES.

Invitation to join. *Law student Richard D. Gilliam Jr. received this Raven Society bid in May 1923.*

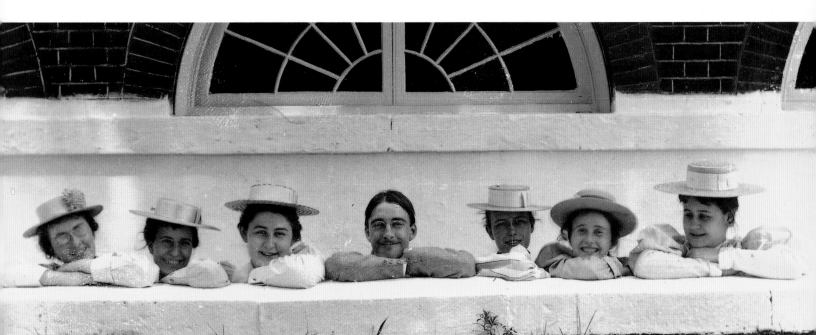

Philip Francis du Pont, alumnus and benefactor. *Great-grandson of the founder of the E. I. du Pont de Nemours Powder Company, precursor to today's DuPont, Philip Francis du Pont attended the University of Virginia from 1897 to 1900. He worked on the yearbook and the literary magazine but was expelled for "neglect of duty." Nevertheless, du Pont remained loyal to the university. Having learned that the largest individual bequest ever made to a college was $3 million, du Pont secretly established a $6-million perpetual trust, valued at $150 million in the late 1990s.*

Members of some social clubs donned offbeat costumes. The Hot Feet Society dressed in devilish garb and crowned a king every year. In 1911 the faculty banned the Hot Feet, declaring that they tended to "promote disorder." They rose again, reincarnated as the IMP Society, still evident today in the stenciled white signature on buildings around the grounds.

The law club, Phi Delta Phi, staged annual "goatings," in which students caricatured professors mercilessly. The 1906 event staged a meeting between benefactor Andrew Carnegie, dressed in a kilt; "Carrie Nation" Dunnington, a faculty wife known for pious temperance; and the "Easter girl," a campus sweetheart—all roles filled by male law students.

Easter season was the high point of the social year. There was nothing religious about the date. In fact, celebrations usually attached themselves to Jefferson's birthday, 13 April, always an occasion for ceremony and speakers. As far back as the 1860s, 13 April presented an occasion for mischief as well. In 1869 the *Virginia University Magazine* reported 13 April as the anniversary of the Ugly Club—that year not "as ugly as in previous years," since "the club of last session monopolized the stock of ugliness which should have served the club for several years to come."

Beauty arrived in the form of female companions. "Certainly in my day and generation," wrote alumnus James P. C. Southall, who attended the university in the 1890s, "a student was a hopeless bookworm and an odd fellow indeed who did not have a sweetheart in a bower close enough for him to get a glimpse of her nearly every day, and to take her to church on Sunday." "'Calico' was one pastime common to all students, whether grinds, sports or bums," alumnus Lewis W. Williams remembered. The term originated, Southall wrote, "after the end of the Civil War when for some years (so it is said) young ladies

UNIVERSITY OF VIRGINIA
Overseas Song Book

On the front lines. *During World War I, ties stayed strong between soldiers on the European front and the university. President Alderman sent a Christmas card to students and alumni at war.*

World War I on the Lawn. *In 1917 "the University turned its academic spaces into training camps," wrote the librarian John S. Patton. The War Department sent more than one thousand men as part of the Students' Army Training Corps, shown here assembled on the Lawn.*

James R. McConnell, alumnus and war hero. *A student leader, entering in 1907, McConnell enlisted in the Lafayette Escadrille, an American fleet of biplanes. He painted a red foot on his airplane in memory of his days as king of the Hot Feet. McConnell was shot down in March 1917 during air battle over Alsace and in 1919 was commemorated by the sculpture of Icarus (opposite), created by Gutzon Borglum for the university.*

in Virginia had to be content to wear calico frocks because their sires could not afford to buy silks and satins for them." Those most eager for female companionship were called "calicoists."

Bright party lights strained the power capacity of the university in 1906. "DINAMO TAXED," read a notice in *College Topics.* "All persons attending the germans, whether dancers or onlookers, are urgently required to turn out the lights in their rooms, as the power house will be surely taxed by the electrical display for the germans."

The Great War

In March 1917, as war grew imminent, the university petitioned to instate military training on the grounds. Students enrolled in such courses as military science and tactics or telegraphy, telephony, and searchlights. The Reserve Officers' Training Corps—a new concept—began two days before the United States declared war, and eight out of ten students applied. Drills on university grounds began a week later. More than one thousand new students arrived as part of the Students' Army Training Corps.

Twenty-six faculty members turned from teaching to the war effort. Law professor Armistead M. Dobie served as aide to Major General Adelbert Cronkhite and as chief of military intelligence publications,

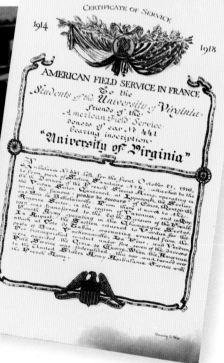

Ambulance units in France. *In the university's first organized response to the war effort, two companies of men formed ambulance units. They traveled to France in 1917, meeting heavy fire and receiving American Field Service commendations.*

111

Fifty-year reunion at the centennial. *These members of the Civil War–era class of 1861 were among the more than eight hundred alumni who returned to the university to join in the celebration of its centennial. They received a medal of honor (below) from their alma mater.*

stationed in France, for over two years. Astronomy professor Samuel A. Mitchell was named director of the School of Navigation for the U.S. Shipping Board. Physics professor Llewellyn G. Hoxton improved aviation engines for the Bureau of Standards.

Alumni organized the University of Virginia Base Hospital No. 41; 25 medical officers, 100 nurses, and more than 150 other enlistees rendered emergency assistance at Saint-Denis, near Paris. Another troop of 72 Virginia men volunteered together for ambulance service, sailing to France in 1917. So many Virginia men were stationed in Europe that the university established London and Paris bureaus, where students and alumni could gather. On Founder's Day, 13 April 1918, alumni in Europe wired Alderman with "affectionate Founder's Day Greetings."

In all, more than 2,500 students and alumni served during World War I. Eighty gave their lives, including a popular student named James Rogers McConnell, who had been yearbook editor and king of the Hot Feet in 1910. Even before the United States entered the war, McConnell joined the Lafayette Escadrille. Shot down by German fighter planes, he was commemorated with a memorial in the small French town where he fell as well as with the 1919 statue of Icarus that now stands between Alderman and Clemons Libraries.

A Growing University

Ten years into his presidency, Alderman told the Board of Visitors that the university was experiencing "growth and development," but not, he assured them, "in hysterical ways." Between 1904 and 1929 the faculty grew from 48 to 290; student numbers increased from 500 to 2,450. Annual income, endowment, and state appropriations increased. During Alderman's first year in office, 1904 to 1905, the university operated in the red; by 1930 the annual budget had grown more than ten times and the endowment had grown to ten million dollars.

In 1919 Sidney Fiske Kimball joined the university faculty as its first professor of architecture. Students of art and architecture studied together, following the method of the École des Beaux Arts in Paris. "We had to learn to draw, to use watercolors," says Floyd E. Johnson, who received a bachelor's degree in architecture in 1934. "It taught you to see." For final projects architecture students stayed up all night, solving the same problems that

Beaux Arts Ball. *In the 1920s architecture students began hosting a costume gala, named for the Beaux Arts tradition of architectural training. The Beaux Arts Ball continued as an annual masquerade (top, ca. 1950) through the twentieth century.*

Beaux Arts students around the world were tackling that year. Students created huge ink-and-wash renderings of historical details from European architectural traditions. Johnson recalls that he and fellow students kept a mason jar of grain alcohol near the drawing board, using the alcohol to create distinctive wash effects.

Edmund S. Campbell, an architect and watercolorist, continued the Beaux Arts tradition at Virginia after Kimball left to head the Philadelphia Museum of Art. In the 1950s the Beaux Arts tradition faded as modernism overtook American architecture, but students still worked around the clock on major projects. Often projects had to be completed in a given time span, intensifying the pressure but replicating the demands of the architecture

Homage to the founder. *As part of a four-day celebration of the university's centennial, an allegorical pageant titled "The Shadow of the Builder" was performed on the steps of the Rotunda (above and opposite). It dramatized in dance and verse Jefferson's decision to use fine Italian marble instead of rough Virginia stone for the column capitals of the Rotunda.*

profession. The tradition's influence continued through the twentieth century as well in the Beaux Arts Ball, a fantastic costumed event organized by architecture students, held sporadically from the 1920s on and annually since 1973.

Celebrating the Centennial

While all eyes were on the war, the university reached its centennial year, dating from the first Board of Visitors meeting on 29 March 1819. Officials planned a spectacular four-day event, albeit two years late, to coincide with the final exercises of 1921. Vacated army barracks housed eight hundred visiting alumni; cots for two hundred more lined Jefferson and Washington Halls. Dignitaries from universities around the world joined delegates from across America to honor the university. More than one hundred automobiles made a modern-day pilgrimage to Monticello, where Jefferson Levy opened the doors to what was then his private home. Faculty and students, community members, and dance students from Mississippi performed a pageant written for the occasion, "The Shadow of the Builder."

English professors John C. Metcalf and James Southall Wilson invited writers to contribute poetry to a centennial anthology. The resulting volume, *The Enchanted Years,* gathers verse from many now-unknown authors with works contributed by Thomas Hardy, D. H. Lawrence, Vachel Lindsay, and Edwin Arlington Robinson. To further celebrate, the alumni association commissioned alumnus Philip A. Bruce to write a history of the university. In five volumes, published between 1920 and 1922, Bruce brought together facts, anecdotes, and his own observations, culminating in an epic that he considered told a salient story of the South. "If we had no other means of gauging the spirit of those States," wrote Bruce in his conclusion, "and the general conditions, which, from generation to generation, have prevailed within their borders, we would not be entirely lacking in light upon these subjects so long as we possessed the story of the University of Virginia."

ATHLETICS

Exercise seems not to have been important to the university's early students. Fencing lessons were offered privately in the initial years, and pugilistic sports like boxing and wielding the broad sword were taught in the 1840s, but the first true physical education came from "roly poly" J. E. D'Alfonce, Polish by birth but French to his students (who called him Monsieur). In 1852 D'Alfonce taught in a gymnasium where, according to one student, "three hundred men squat li toads hopping along with tickl gravity towards some imagin; pond, to the sound of 'one, two, tree, four.'" The Civil War interrupted such activities.

Virginia's first athletic team was the rowing crew, which competed for a few years in the late nineteenth century, until river condi-

Above: Football hero Bill Dudley.
Left: Boxing coach H. Hosen.

tions made practice difficult and the team disbanded. The Rivanna reservoir, built in 1967, guaranteed smooth, deep practice waters, so students began rowing again. A women's crew formed in 1974; in 1995 that team began varsity competition. In 1996 the university opened its new Thomas Temple Allan Boathouse on the reservoir.

In the 1890s a football team practiced where Brooks Hall now stands, and it traveled to pit its skills against Penn, Princeton, and Washington and Lee. "There were goals, and there were captains, but few, if any, regulations," wrote a faculty member of the day. Coach Johnny Poe trained his football players with a vengeance. During one scrimmage he ran with the ball and "instructed the players forthwith to pile up on him," wrote player Murray McGuire. Out of respect, they jumped gingerly on him. "He expressed the greatest dissatisfaction," recalled McGuire, "and yelled at the top of his voice that no one was on his head." In 1909, however, after the Virginia halfback Archer Christian died of a concussion, President Alderman and the director of athletics, William Lambeth, crusaded nationally for stricter rules in football. Although they advocated

Above: George Welsh and football players, ca. 1990. Right: Coach "Pop" Lannigan and basketball players, ca. 1920.

headgear, a rule requiring helmets did not come into force until 1939.

McGuire spearheaded the effort to build a better playing field, complaining that the area northeast of the Rotunda was cramped and full of rocks, which tended to destroy balls, tear up uniforms, and injure players. Lambeth Field, built in 1901 and soon enhanced with a colonnaded amphitheater for spectators, hosted athletic events into the 1970s. In its heyday it served as the university's football field, baseball diamond, and track.

Six-foot-five Eppa Rixey, who studied chemistry and Latin at the university, starred in tennis, golf, and basketball, but he excelled in baseball, as a left-handed pitcher. He joined the Philadelphia Phillies in 1914 and later played for the Cincinnati Reds. In 1963 he was inducted in the Baseball Hall of Fame, the only ACC player to win that honor.

In 1922 Johnny LaRowe, owner of a popular billiard parlor on the Corner, started coaching boxing. Soon LaRowe, "more interested in making men than boxers," led the team to national prominence, drawing hundreds of spectators to matches first in Old Cabell Hall then in Memorial Gymnasium, which opened in 1924. LaRowe continued to coach even after being confined to a wheelchair. His biggest star, Adolph Leftwich, boxed on the U.S. Olympic team.

From 1939 to 1941, Bill Dudley drew national attention as captain of a winning football team. "It was before the age of specialization, and he could do it all," recalls Gilbert H. Sullivan, a former director of the university's alumni association. "He punted, he kicked extra points and field goals, he was a great ball carrier, a good blocker. You could see the fire." After the war, football teams posted more successes, beating Harvard 47-0 in 1947. That game made history for another reason, as Harvard player

HOW **CAN** YOU MISS
THIS ??
VIRGINIA
VS
VANDERBILT
LAMBETH FIELD
CHARLOTTESVILLE
NOVEMBER 1, 1913.

MEET ME AT THE CORNER ← Carl Zeisberg →

Chester Pierce became the first African American to play football at the University of Virginia.

From the early 1950s on, University of Virginia football slumped, with one winning season (1968) in thirty years. Star players—James Bakhtiar, Robert Canevari, David Sloan—gained the admiration of their fellow students, but football fans enjoyed few wins until George Welsh started coaching in 1981.

That same year, Bruce Arena began coaching men's soccer, leading the team into the 1990s with a record-breaking streak of successes. In 1992 and 1993, playing in the university's new Klöckner Stadium, the soccer team enjoyed winning seasons, but the climax season came in 1994. Forward A. J. Wood scored the winning goal against Indiana—the only point scored in the game—and the Cavaliers became the first soccer team in history to win the NCAA championship four years in a row.

Beloved coach H. H. "Pop" Lannigan, at the university from 1905 until his death in 1930, brought the sport of basketball with him from Cornell. Virginia won the first game it played, against the Charlottesville YMCA in 1906. In 1941 the basketball team played City College of New York in the National Invitational Tournament, its first postseason appearance ever. In the 1970s and 1980s, men's basketball teams advanced, and a Virginia women's basketball team started up with a winning season in 1973–74.

By 1973, three years after coeducation was fully instated in the College of Arts and Sciences, the university supported two other varsity women's teams, field hockey and tennis. By 1998, twelve women's varsity teams were competing. Mary Brundage, the university's first female athlete, competed alongside male swimmers on the varsity team in 1966. In 1977 cross-country runner Margaret

Groos became the first woman to receive an athletic grant-in-aid from the university, and at one point Groos held the Virginia record for every long-distance event. Many other women athletes from the university have gone on to gain recognition. Valerie Ackerman, for example, a star basketball player of the 1970s, in 1995 became the first president of the Women's National Basketball Association, an affiliate of the NBA.

The issue of balance between academics and athletics has concerned university staff and administrators throughout the twentieth century. The General Athletic Association managed all sporting activities at the turn of the century, but President Alderman established further controls, stressing academic achievement. In 1952 the influence of "big-time athletics" was questioned in the controversial Gooch Report, written by a committee under the leadership of a political science professor named Robert K. Gooch, who as a football quarterback in 1914 and 1915 had led Virginia's team through two shutout seasons. The Gooch Report recommended that football and athletic scholarships be abolished. The university did not follow those recommendations, but that report became the first of many self-examinations by which officials tried to ensure that athletic prominence did not compromise academic standards.

Basketball players Heidi and Heather Burge, 1993

ACC champions, 1996

Through Hard Times

John Lloyd Newcomb, second president of the university

During the 1920s the academic year began with a gathering of the full student body and faculty. All-university gatherings continued periodically throughout the year. Dr. Alderman (as students called him, although he had no doctorate degree) hosted a monthly "College Hour," inviting speakers to address issues of university concern. Although he dwelt on university finances, Alderman himself was a rousing speaker, recalled the French author Julian Green, a student at Virginia in the 1920s:

Like everyone else at the University, I received a notification to attend the inaugural meeting of the academic year at Cabell Hall.... How many were we? Perhaps eight hundred. The teaching staff in their gowns and mortar-boards gathered on stage.... Our President certainly looked impressive. Tall, thin and greying, he wore a pince-nez with a tortoise-shell frame which would fall off each time his nose twitched and cause one to start every time it happened.... Nature had blessed him with a superb voice which he used wisely, whether he was exalting the fine history of the University, which he always referred to as "this institution of learning"; or whether, with eloquent circumlocutions whose meaning became increasingly clear,

1940

- **2,600 students**

- **200 faculty members**

- **18,000 alumni**

- **Tuition: $110 for Virginians; $310 for non-Virginians**

- **Lawn and Range rooms: $125 per year**

- **Meals at the Commons: $28.50 per month**

- **The Virginia Spectator, 20¢ a copy, $2 annually (20 issues)**

Madison Hall, home of the first college YMCA. *Built in 1905, Madison Hall began as headquarters for America's first campus-based chapter of the Young Men's Christian Association, but it slowly evolved into a student union building. By the late 1970s it housed university administrative offices, including the president's.*

The Dry Dock. *A soda fountain opened in 1943 in the basement of Madison Hall, called by Virginius Dabney "the first thing remotely describable as a student union that the university had ever had."*

he reminded us that the University was badly in need of money, at which precise point the pince-nez would fall off.

Mrs. A. E. Walker. *Dubbed the "Queen of Madison Hall," Mrs. Walker (left) served as hostess at the YMCA, where she served tea to students on Sundays at five.* Alumni News *celebrated her tradition of "friendship and something like other-mothership," writing that "she has been pouring it ever since, the tea and the charm."*

At Madison Hall, Mrs. A. E. Walker served Sunday tea at five. She was hired in 1918, so *Alumni News* reported on the twenty-fifth anniversary of that date, to provide "the feminine touch" to an all-male university. Madison Hall had been built by the YMCA, but in 1934 the university began leasing the building and broadened its use as a student union. "The variety dances presented at nominal charges have attracted hundreds of students each night," wrote *Corks and Curls* in 1934. "The club room, with its lounges, radio, newspapers and big log fire, is gaining popularity daily." Student publications and the student senate had offices in Madison Hall. In 1943 the Dry Dock soda fountain opened in the basement.

The First Women

By the 1920s two-thirds of all American colleges and universities were coeducational. Yale University was accepting women into its graduate programs. The question of whether to admit women to the University of Virginia was bound to arise.

Thirty years before, in 1893, Caroline Preston Davis had been granted permission to take an examination in mathematics. She was awarded a certificate, equivalent to those received by male students at the university. Her case sparked considerable discussion as to how to make a place for women at the University of Virginia, but ultimately the Board of Visitors decided that the university would neither enroll nor examine female candidates for certification, since "admission of women would be unwise and injurious to the best interests of the University."

In 1901 four women enrolled in the university's new two-year training program for nurses in the medical school. Designed strictly for women, the nursing program was entirely separate from the rest of the university. Participants received no

The first University of Virginia women. *The first women to study at the university were "pupil nurses," who worked twelve-hour days in the hospital ward, learning primarily through a grueling apprenticeship. At right is Alice Leathers Maddex, in the first class of pupil nurses, 1901. The demands of World War I forced a reconsideration of nursing education at the university and elsewhere. By the 1920s, nurse training combined study with practice.*

Women as guests. *Women may have attended the university as graduate and professional students from 1920 on, but from the vantage point of most undergraduates, women's presence was noticed most when they arrived by train for party weekends. At right, the popular cartoonist Carl Zeisberg captured the complex feelings of students and alumni at the University of Virginia when the decision was made in 1920 to admit women to graduate and professional schools.*

college credit or degrees, only diplomas for two years of apprenticeship, during which they provided an essential workforce for the growing hospital. At first nursing students roomed on the top floor of the hospital; but as their numbers grew, they lived in Randall Hall, then in McKim Hall, built for them in 1931.

By 1916 in Virginia, only Randolph-Macon Woman's College offered the equivalent of a four-year college degree to women. Otherwise, women attended normal schools in Farmville, Harrisonburg, Radford, and Fredericksburg that offered abbreviated schooling for future teachers. Mary Branche-Cooke Munford, the Richmond widow of a state senator, took up the cause, fired with "an almost passionate desire" to convince the legislature to admit women to the University of Virginia. President Alderman supported the notion of a coordinate college on the model of Radcliffe at Harvard, but he denounced "frank co-education." In 1916, witnessed by "the largest crowd that has ever shouldered its way into galleries, onto the floor, the aisles and even the cloakroom," according to the *Richmond Times-Dispatch,* the House of Delegates defeated by two votes a bill that would have established a university-affiliated coordinate college for women.

After the war Mary Munford pressed on. When the College of William and Mary became coeducational in 1918, she called it "the sop the legislature threw to us to keep us quiet" and kept her sights on the University of Virginia. In 1920 the Board of Visitors agreed to admit women, aged twenty and over, to the graduate and professional schools. Three women attained the master of arts degree in 1921; three women enrolled in law classes in 1921, one of whom, Elizabeth H. Tompkins, in 1923 became the first woman to graduate with a law degree from the university.

It took great strength for a woman to choose to attend the University of Virginia in those early years. Writing years later, Dr. Margaret M. Glendy, who received her M.D. degree in 1931, recalled that when she applied for admission, "I knew that no one ever spoke to coeds." To support the small contingent of women students, the university appointed a dean of women in 1927. In 1934 Roberta Hollingsworth, a 1933 Virginia Ph.D. in Romance languages, became dean of women, a post she held until 1967.

Through the 1930s and 1940s, up to two hundred women enrolled at

the university each year, primarily in education and the graduate departments in arts and sciences, but always a few in engineering, law, and medicine. In 1943, Mary Washington College in Fredericksburg was designated the University of Virginia's coordinate women's college, and third-year women could transfer into the

Elizabeth H. Tompkins, first female law graduate. *Two women entered the law school in 1921 and passed the bar at the end of that academic year. One went directly into legal practice; the other, Elizabeth Tompkins, returned to school and completed a law degree in 1923. "Her powers of acquisition and of appreciation of legal principles were fully equal to those of the men in the front rank of the graduating class," reported her dean to President Alderman.*

Despite the efforts of students and alumni to check it co-education was forced upon the University. Now the tendency is to accept it with a shrug, and say that "after all it isn't so bad."

— CORKS AND CURLS, *1925*

The*Virginia* Quarterly Review

Since 1925 the University of Virginia has housed the Virginia Quarterly Review, *a periodical of literature and social commentary. The VQR's founding editor was James Southall Wilson, a professor of English. Editors since have included Stringfellow Barr, Charlotte Kohler, and Staige Blackford Jr. Among the articles that first appeared in the* Virginia Quarterly Review *are the following:*

D. H. Lawrence
"The Bogey between the Generations"
(1929)

T. S. Eliot
"Personality and Demonic Possession"
(1934)

Thomas Mann
"Thoughts on Nazi Germany"
(1941)

Jean-Paul Sartre
"We Write for Our Own Time"
(1947)

Bertrand Russell
"George Bernard Shaw"
(1951)

Henry Steele Commager
"Do We Have a Class Society?"
(1961)

Robert Graves
"How to Hold the Reader's Attention"
(1968)

Influential women. *Two students join the dean of women Roberta Hollingsworth, at center, in admiring a portrait of Mary Munford. Long an advocate for female students at the university, Munford led the political battle that resulted in the admission of women into graduate and professional schools in 1920. She served on the Board of Visitors from 1926 until her death in 1938.*

Roberta Hollingsworth Gwathmey, dean of women. *Although not the first dean of women, Roberta Hollingsworth Gwathmey held that post the longest, from 1934 until 1967. She was the first woman to receive a doctoral degree in Romance languages from the University of Virginia, in 1933. She established the Co-Ed Room, where women could gather socially, and she campaigned for the construction of a women's dormitory.*

College of Arts and Sciences if they wished to study subjects not offered at Mary Washington.

Dean Hollingsworth greeted all women at the beginning of the year, presenting a handbook in which she exhorted them to remain "as inconspicuous as possible on the grounds and at The Corner." "The history of women students here is brief in comparison with the history of the University as an institution," wrote Hollingsworth, "and never let it be said that co-education has weakened the University, but rather that it has contributed to its prestige." Women students gathered each afternoon at the Co-Ed Room on the West Range for tea, served by Betty Slaughter, a beloved housekeeper, who came to be known as "Betty Co-Ed."

Julian Green, French author and alumnus. *In 1919 Green's American parents, having moved to France for business, sent their son to the University of Virginia. He completed three years of college then returned to France for the rest of his life, distinguishing himself as a novelist, playwright, and memoirist whose works are much better known in Europe than in the United States. Green was the first American—indeed the first foreigner—to be elected into the highly selective Académie Française. He died in 1998 at the age of ninety-seven.*

President Newcomb

Stricken with tuberculosis in 1914, President Alderman had taken an eighteen-month leave from the university and had left John Lloyd Newcomb, an alumnus and professor in civil engineering, in charge. Newcomb served both as dean of engineering and as assistant to Alderman during the 1920s, orchestrating the centennial celebration and campaigning hard when the state legislature threatened to relocate the medical school to Richmond. Alderman's health never fully returned, so for years Newcomb unofficially bore much of the responsibility of running the university. Yet when Alderman died in 1931, the Board of Visitors took two and a half years to elect the next president.

As the third school year opened without a president, students, faculty, and alumni publicized their support for Newcomb. "Elect a President!" a Richmond newspaper put in bold print. A Norfolk editorial argued that the university "needs no money-hunter, no go-getter, no mere builder

John Lloyd Newcomb. *A civil engineer, Newcomb had managed the university since 1914, when President Alderman departed for months at a time to undergo tuberculosis treatment. Formally inaugurated in 1933, Newcomb was known for his analytical approach, which carried the university through the Great Depression and World War II.*

Paul G. McIntire, university benefactor. *The university landscape changed tremendously during the 1920s through the generosity of Charlottesville native and alumnus Paul G. McIntire, who made his fortune in the Chicago and New York stock markets. Through McIntire's benevolence, the university built an amphitheater just beyond the Lawn (at left), where from 1921 on, final exercises, speeches, and concerts took place. McIntire also underwrote the creation of a school of business and finance. The music department, the amphitheater, and the commerce school still bear his name.*

of buildings and of matriculation lists" but simply "a man who loved the University."

In 1932 Newcomb was finally named the second president of the University of Virginia. Small, shy, and averse to public speaking, he was not a charismatic figure like Edwin Alderman. He brought to the office an engineer's mind for figures and analysis. He could multiply four-digit numbers in his head, and "he knew every length of pipe and foot of material in every building in the University," recalled Joseph L. Vaughan, who began teaching English to engineering students when Newcomb was dean.

Depression Years

Newcomb carried the University of Virginia through the Great Depression and World War II. Faculty salaries dropped 20 percent, but no professor was laid off. In 1934 and 1935, close to three hundred students were supported by National Youth Administration funds, which paid forty or fifty cents an hour for such part-time jobs as research assistant, campus janitor,

The new law building. *Law classes moved in 1932 from Minor Hall to Clark Hall, built thanks to a gift from alumnus William Andrews Clark Jr. One entered Clark Hall through an elegant lobby lit by a skylight and decorated with larger-than-life-sized murals representing the Mosaic and Roman elements of American jurisprudence.*

and campus policeman. Family circumstances forced some students to leave the university, while others worked to stay enrolled.

"My family didn't fare well in the Depression and, beginning in 1930 on, I became literally self-supporting," says George C. Seward, at the university from 1929 to 1936 and earning a bachelor's and a law degree. Seward waited on tables at one boardinghouse, stoked the furnace and recruited renters at another, baby-sat, graded papers, and finally worked his way up on the staff of the Commons dining hall.

The university continued to grow despite the depression. The level of private giving to Virginia did not drop as precipitously as that to northeastern schools. Thanks to private gifts, the university added a law building (Clark Hall), a chemistry building (Cobb Hall), and an athletic field (Scott Stadium). Federal money supplemented a hundred-thousand-dollar gift from Mrs. Evelyn May Bayly Tiffany for an art museum: the Thomas H. Bayly Art Museum opened during graduation week 1934. Private funds and PWA money built new medical facilities as well, so that by 1941 three more hospital buildings had been erected.

William Thornton, for fifty years a leader of engineering education at the university, just survived to see the grand opening of the building that bore his name. He died two weeks after it opened, in 1935. A professor of applied mathematics and chair of the faculty, Thornton had built up the collection of technical equipment—steam engine, boiler, and dynamo—housed in the Rotunda Annex, which was almost entirely destroyed by the fire. Alderman appointed him as the first dean of engineering, and Thornton's deep regard for the liberal arts and the classics influenced his educational vision.

"He was the undisputed intellectual leader of our community," wrote Joseph L. Vaughan, humanities professor and the university's first provost, of Thornton in his book *Rotunda Tales*. "In some ways he was the engineering department.... Men who studied under him came away learning one great lesson, and that was to think and calculate for themselves."

Scott Stadium, 1931. *Athletic events moved from Lambeth Field to Scott Stadium, which was built through the generosity of Frederic W. Scott, a member of the Board of Visitors, who contributed $300,000 for the purpose in 1930.*

The study of engineering. *Under William Thornton's leadership, engineering studies expanded to include a number of different fields. Civil engineering had been offered at the university since the 1830s, but by 1910 the university offered courses in mechanical, electrical, and chemical engineering as well. Drafting classes took place in the Mechanical Laboratory (now Cocke Hall), dedicated to engineering education until Thornton Hall opened in 1935.*

Vaughan himself entered the university as an undergraduate in 1923. He taught a special section of first-year English for engineering students in 1927, and in 1932 the engineering dean Walter S. Rodman appointed Vaughan as head of a new English department within the engineering school, incorporating literature, writing, and ethics centrally into the curriculum, a distinctive element of Virginia's engineering education that continued through the twentieth century.

Crowning the construction that went on during the 1930s, Alderman Library opened with ceremony in 1938. Even as expanded by Stanford White, the Rotunda Dome Room could not accommodate the library's growth; many volumes had to be stored elsewhere. In his last public address, on Founder's Day, 13 April 1931, Alderman had identified a "great library building" as the university's "supreme requirement." The university librarian Harry Clemons kept that vision alive, often quoting Alderman's belief that the library is "the beating heart of the University." When Alderman Library opened, assistant librarian Mary Louise Dinwiddie carried in its first book: Alderman's memorial address in honor of Woodrow Wilson.

A year later, in 1939, the library's McGregor Room opened, an elegant space for the storage and study of rare books. In 1925 Tracy W. McGregor, a Detroit railroad magnate, had bequeathed to the university his collection of books and manuscripts on New World history, including a letter announcing the results of Columbus's first voyage; John Smith's first printed account of the Virginia colony; and Thomas Jefferson's annotated copy of his work *Notes on the State of Virginia*. McGregor's gift greatly advanced efforts to build the library's collection of rare books and manuscripts. The librarian John C. Wyllie culled materials moved from the Rotunda into Alderman Library, separating for special care those that could be considered rare and valuable. With further gifts in the 1920s and 1930s, the university's special collections continued to grow.

Another World War

With the immediacy of Great Depression–era hardships aggravated by prospects of another world war, more serious issues began to punctuate on-grounds dialogues. The 1938 *Virginia Reel* referred to Hitler, questioning "what he's going to do to the *Universität* after the *Anschluss mit dem deutschen Reich.*" In the 1940 *Spectator*, articles on honors courses and graduate-student life—and an earnest discussion of sexuality among college students, written by a local psychiatrist—outweighed chatty pieces about drinking and getting away with little work. By 1943, as students watched their classmates go to war, the university indulged in only a "Little Easter Week," and the spring formal ended not with "The Good Old Song" but with the national anthem.

In May 1940 President Roosevelt addressed graduates, including his son, Franklin Delano Roosevelt Jr., who was receiving a law degree. Just that morning Roosevelt had learned that Mussolini had attacked France. "On this tenth day of June, 1940, the hand that held the dagger has struck

Graduation address, 1940. *Speaking to graduates in Memorial Gymnasium (a rainstorm drove the ceremony inside), Franklin Delano Roosevelt at the last minute added an announcement of the Italian invasion of France, which had taken place earlier that day.*

Men in uniform. *After Pearl Harbor, more young men on grounds wore uniforms. By spring 1943, three in four students had enlisted in the military. As soldiers were sent overseas, the proportion of women students and laboratory technicians increased— a harbinger of the growth to come in the number of women at the university.*

it into the back of its neighbor," he announced to the graduation crowd. "Once more the future of the nation and of the American people is at stake."

Immediately after the Japanese attack on Pearl Harbor, in December 1941, enrollments began to fall. In 1942 the law school enrolled 56 students, a fraction of its normal 350. The total number of students at the university dropped by two-thirds in five years, from over 3,000 in 1939 to 1,322 in 1944. "Everything here was oriented toward the military," says O. Allan Gianniny, an engineering professor who entered the university as an

Seamen on grounds. *A group of university students volunteered first in the state and early in the nation for the navy's "V" (for "volunteer") classes. By early 1943, V-1, V-5, V-7, and V-12 classes had been activated at the university. Volunteers remained in the classroom, although they were ready for action if the war demanded.*

undergraduate in 1942. "On the grounds, the only people we saw as civilians had some sort of physical handicap." As men went overseas, the proportion of women among enrolled students rose, to 18 percent in 1945. Many women students focused on the war effort as well, however. The engineering school instituted a tuition-free ten-week course to qualify women for civil service posts as junior engineers.

"Everyone wanted to be in uniform of some sort," remembers Frank L. Hereford Jr., who graduated in 1943 and continued in graduate studies in physics, later to become university president. Hundreds of students volunteered for Dawn Patrol, a student-initiated early morning preinduction battalion renamed Dusk Patrol when exercises moved to evening hours. Some volunteered for naval service, becoming classified as "V-1," "V-5," "V-7," or "V-12" and allowed to continue their studies until called into active duty. The air force established a course in meteorology, and the army instituted a School of Military Government at the university to train leaders for combat in regions coming under Allied control. The change was so dramatic, and so typical of the times, that the *New York Times* ran an article entitled "War Changes the Face of the Campus" in November 1942, illustrating it with a photograph of ROTC drills in front of the Rotunda.

Alumni News filled with photos of uniformed men. Class notes tracked the whereabouts of enlisted men and officers, such as Admiral William F. "Bull" Halsey, commander in chief in the South Pacific, and Lieutenant General Alexander A. Vandegrift, marine commander of the invasion at Guadalcanal, both University of Virginia students at the turn of the century. Indeed, *Alumni News* reported that most Virginia alumni serving were officers. More than 5,000 University of Virginia alumni served in the armed forces during World War II; 139 were decorated for distinguished service; 134 died.

Faculty at the university mobilized as well. As school began in 1943, 45 out of 215 faculty had taken leave for military or diplomatic duty. Medical professor Staige D. Blackford led the Eighth Evacuation Hospital unit—31 men and 24 women from Virginia, joined by another 38 workers who called themselves "illegitimate sons and daughters of the University." The unit cared for tens of thousands of wounded in North Africa and Italy. On 13 April 1943, Blackford wrote to Newcomb from "somewhere in North Africa," telling him of their impromptu Founder's Day celebration.

At home, Alderman Library served as a safe haven for Library of Congress holdings. At first, says Francis L. Berkeley Jr., they sent only rare items, like the Magna Carta, the Constitution, and the papers of the first presidents. Soon, however, more vans were coming in the dark of night, bringing several million documents—the papers of the presidents all the way through to Woodrow Wilson—to Alderman Library. That arrangement proved so satisfactory

Edward Stettinius, alumnus and statesman. *White-haired even as a student, Stettinius was known for his missionary efforts. "While other students were going into the Ragged Mountains only to fill up their Mason Jars," College Topics claimed, "Ed was devoting his inexhaustible energy to converting the heathen of the region." Stettinius served as secretary of state under Roosevelt and ran the Lend-Lease Administration, which used aid and equipment to secure the allegiance of nations including Egypt, China, Russia, and Iran. After serving as representative to the United Nations, he became university rector in 1946.*

A wartime Founder's Day request. *When President Newcomb received this telegram, he responded, invoking Thomas Jefferson: "To the millions of devoted men and women now engaged in the greatest struggle in human history he would say that he fought on a shorter front, but that it was identically the same battle, nonetheless."*

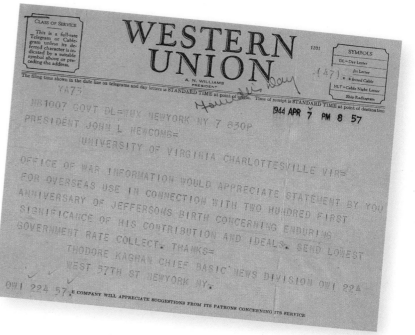

Copeley Hill, a new neighborhood. *To accommodate returning veterans and their families, the university bought war surplus trailers and built makeshift apartment buildings on a tract north of the grounds called Copeley Hill.*

that soon the entire Union Catalog, drawers and drawers of index cards representing every printed work held by any U.S. library, filled Alderman's third-floor stacks, covered with tarps to obscure their significance.

After the War

With the end of the war came a new kind of student, thanks to the Servicemen's Readjustment Act of 1944—known as the G.I. Bill—which paid tuition for over two million returning veterans nationwide. By October 1946 more than 3,300 veterans and $1,250,000 in G.I. Bill funds had come to the University of Virginia. "Veterans outnumber non-veterans by large majorities in all departments of the University," reported *College Topics*.

The character of this incoming class was different from that of those before. Older male students, husbands and fathers, returned from the armed services with career-minded determination. Housing for families, not just single men, was needed, and in volume, fast. The university set up three-room war-surplus trailers on a grassy 120-acre site northwest of the grounds. By 1950, Copeley Hill had developed into a new sort of university community, housing over a thousand people in a makeshift family neighborhood, with streets and streetlights, a governing council and a mayor, a newsletter, a grocery, a kindergarten, and a baby-sitting association.

In some ways, the university could return to education as usual, but in other ways it would never be the same. Student organizations, from fraternities to honor societies to student government, had lost their momentum. Student publications had skipped issues or had shrunk in size. Traditions had weakened, and the new generation of students would test what of the past was to survive.

Class of 1948. *The graduating class of 1948 was the largest ever, with men returning from war, using the G.I. Bill to fund their educations. Here, during graduation, Frank Crenshaw, president of his class, presents funds toward a memorial tablet honoring those lost in World War II.*

The Corner

In 1860 the women of Charlottesville raised money to build a walkway between the town and the university; before that there had been nothing but a muddy footpath. The new walk led to the northeast edge of the university grounds, a square corner of land below West Range and Washington Hall, where the Washington Debating Society met. At that corner, just outside university limits, the two-story Temperance Hall had been erected in 1855. And at that corner one passed through a simple gate and walked up a tree-lined path toward the Annex and Rotunda.

By the 1880s the Temperance Hall had been transformed into commercial space, owned by the university and leased as income property, with the profits going to support religious activities at the school. A post office and a bookstore moved in, and the words "University Book Store" were painted on the brickwork between the first and second floor. Across the way, from 1876 on, stood a competing bookstore, established by two brothers named Anderson.

In 1913 *College Topics* announced "plans for beautifying the 'Corner' by removing the unsightly building now occupied by the post office and Olivier's book store and by erecting a new building on their present site." Plans included a new gateway at the foot of the "long walk" up the hill toward the West Range and the Rotunda. Mrs. Charles H. Senff, the widow of an alumnus, gave two thousand dollars for a pillared entrance, with tablets inscribed with verses commemorating the tradition of honor.

"The university is attempting to substitute a new corner for the old," a *College Topics* writer grieved. He hoped, however, that change would incite an "innovation spirit" among shopkeepers on the other side of the street. When the new corner building opened in 1914, it held a bookstore, a soda fountain, a post office, and the "most artistic tea room in the South," according to advertisements.

The Corner, ca. 1920. Above right: A postcard of the Corner, looking east toward downtown Charlottesville.

By the early 1920s, business enterprises dominated both sides of the street. A clothing store, a shoe repair, and a bank had opened in the building alongside the ever-popular tea room. Miscalculations were made as the university expanded its medical facilities, so the building was repositioned 150 feet to the east. Later, the building housed Student Health Services and then, when the Elson Student Health Center opened, the Women's Center.

In the 1920s, business was flourishing across the street as well. At the east end of the block, grocer Henry Irving and butcher Harry Robinson ran the University Grocery; at the west end, you could buy cigarettes for $1.19 a carton at Charlottesville's

Left: The Corner, 1890s. Above: The Virginian, longest-serving restaurant on the Corner, 1930s.

first A & P. If doctors wore white coats into Dr. Sam Chancellor's drugstore, he gave them a free sample of Coca-Cola, the newest beverage on the market. At Charlie Zehab's, students sat at oilcloth-covered tables and enjoyed the specialty: a hot dog, piled high with Greek chili, mustard, onions, and catsup, all for just a nickel. African American entrepreneurs Charlie and William Brown ran a two-chair barbershop, one shelf holding labeled shaving mugs for their more august clientele. For relaxation, most students headed to Johnny LaRowe's pool hall. For entertain-

Corner merchants and familiars, ca. 1910, including (at right) barbers Charlie and William Brown, flanking Uncle Henry Martin, the Rotunda bell ringer

ment, the downtown Jefferson Theater was just a streetcar ride away.

Mrs. Ellie Page ran one of many student boardinghouses near the university. In a house located behind the businesses on University Avenue, Mrs. Page accommodated up to forty residents and diners at a time from 1894 to 1954. Students so enjoyed seeing Mrs. Page's young daughter, Ellie Wood Page, ride her pony through the neighborhood that they nailed up a sign naming the road after her. Her mother objected, but students insisted that it was an honor. By

the 1920s new houses had joined Mrs. Page's on the street now officially named Elliewood Avenue.

Throughout the twentieth century, the Corner was the bustling backyard of the university. Faculty, staff, and students met at the Kitch Inn for lunch—cheeseburger, fries, and French apple pie—and at the University Cafeteria for dinner, where Mr. Weber served southern fried chicken, pinto beans, and collard greens. Students played pool at Mr. Van Lear's billiard hall—ten cents a setup in the 1950s. Eljo's and Ed Michtom's sold the clothes that every fashionable Wahoo wanted to wear. They bought their pipes and tobacco by the ounce at Mincer's Humidor, founded in 1948 by Robert W. Mincer, a New York tobacconist and pipe maker.

"Men had just come back from the war, and the sophisticated thing to do was to smoke a pipe," says Bobby Mincer, Robert's son, second of three generations operating the business. There was Mincer's No. 10 (a mild Burley base with Cavendish added) and Mr. Jefferson's (fuller body, with wine-cured tobacco). Some customers, like the humanities professor Bedford Moore, requested their own blends, and Mincer's kept a three-by-five file card for each recipe.

As the university grew in numbers and Charlottesville grew in size, students began to shop and eat elsewhere. Barracks Road Shopping Center, which opened in 1959, displaced Carroll's Tea Room, a favorite drinking hole among students through the 1940s and 1950s, known for its slogan, "No Carroll, No Tea, No Room." Some Corner businesses disappeared; others redefined their market. In 1976, area merchant John Crafaik founded Littlejohn's, a New York–style deli that stayed open twenty-four hours a day. In 1977 a multishop mall opened on Fourteenth Street, taking over the oddly angled space of Page's Florist. Soon, Rising Sun Bakery sold bread, cookies, coffee, and sandwiches from early in the morning until late at night.

University Diner, home of the Grillswith, ca. 1980

Other businesses held fast to tradition. Late-night carousers would go to the White Spot for a Gusburger (named after a customer who devised the recipe): a hamburger topped with cheese and a fried egg. Those with a sweet tooth would order the University Diner's Grillswith: two glazed doughnuts, flipped on the hot grill, then topped with a scoop of vanilla ice cream.

The Virginian had gone through many transformations by 1974, when twenty-four-year-old newcomer Mary Ann Parr bought it. She replaced green linoleum with wooden tables, wooden floors, and, for a bar, a soapstone cadaver table salvaged from the medical school. "We created the sense of its being old," Parr says. Five years later, when Parr replaced the sagging wooden floors, people complained that she was destroying history.

In 1992 the Corner enjoyed a thorough renovation: sidewalks widened and laid with brick, benches and streetlights installed. Together with the Rugby Road neighborhood, the Corner was approved for listing on the Virginia Register of Historic Places.

Yet few remembered how it got its name. In 1977 a *Cavalier Daily* reporter asked local merchants why the neighborhood was called "the Corner." "I guess it's the corner of the university," said Milton Via, who ran a barbershop under the Virginian. "It was probably looked at as the corner of the town," surmised Frank Ferneyhough, manager of the University Bookstore. Bobby Mincer thought it was just a generic phrase, as in "I'm going down to the corner." Attention had long ago shifted away from the corner of university property where the name began, but the Corner remained a vital gathering place for the entire community.

The White Spot, home of the Gusburger, 1984

The Capstone of
Virginia Education

*Colgate Darden,
third president
of the university*

A s the university emerged from the war years, some felt the urge to "recapture the spirit of Virginia of pre-war days," as the 1947 *Corks and Curls* put it. John L. Newcomb had declared that he would leave the presidency in 1947, and the appointment of Colgate W. Darden as third president of the university signaled change. "Those who live in a great tradition," Darden wrote in his 1949 annual report, must beware of "holding a flickering torch before cold altars. Once more an opportunity is here for the University to assist in creating an aristocracy of the intellect."

President Darden

Darden had grown up in the farm country outside Franklin, Virginia. He attended public schools and graduated from the University of Virginia in 1922, serving in World War I during his college years. He attended Oxford University briefly and received a law degree from Columbia. His wife, Constance, was a member of the wealthy du Pont family, and Darden took pride in referring to Jefferson's discussions of educational philosophy with her French ancestor Pierre Samuel du Pont de Nemours.

Darden was a politician. He had already served as a member of the state house of delegates, as a congressman, and as governor. Friends in the legislature wanted him to succeed Senator Carter Glass, but the university presidency, he said later in an interview with the Norfolk journalist Guy Friddell, seemed to him "an infinitely better piece of public work." At first his political connections made faculty suspicious of him, but ultimately

1960

- *4,750 students*

- *580 faculty members*

- *College tuition and fees: $344 for Virginians; $779 for non-Virginians*

- *Lawn and Range rooms: $250–$325 per year*

- *Estimated personal expenses for an undergraduate: $795–$1,110 for nine months*

- *Plume and Sword, 15¢ a copy, $2 annually (20 issues)*

Dean's secretary for forty years. *Miss Mary B. Proffitt comforted students as they waited to face a stern Dean Page or Dean Lewis. "There has always been that 'ain't tellin'' look in her keen smiling eyes and good Scotch mouth," an alumnus recalled. Colgate Darden considered her such an important presence during his student years that he asked her to sign his diploma.*

those connections served the university. When the university needed money, recalls Vincent Shea, bursar under Darden, he would go to Richmond and make a personal call on the state budget director, with whom he had worked as governor. Darden continued to wield influence in Richmond on behalf of the university long after his presidency.

Darden wanted the university to become the "capstone of Virginia's education system." Enrollment jumped briefly as veterans returned from the war, but it slid in the early 1950s. Out-of-state and preparatory school applicants far outnumbered those from Virginia's public schools. In 1954 newly appointed director of admissions Raymond C. Bice reported that of just under 1,000 applications for admission to the College of Arts and Sciences, 632 came from other states, including 342 from out-of-state prep school students.

State U-ism

Even as he entered office, Darden put the fraternities on guard. They knew that as governor he had encouraged William and Mary College to prohibit students from living in fraternity or sorority houses. Students feared he would do something similar at Virginia. In his 1949 annual report, Darden criticized the "enervating influence" of "a group of fraternities and societies dedicated primarily and sometimes exclusively to the outward and visible signs of social distinction."

Student satire. *Irreverent cartoons in the Virginia Spectator expressed student attitudes toward change. Right, an inventive Rotunda beanie. At left, the spectre of a "State U," where masses of students line up to enter a futuristic student union building.*

150

Students and alumni alike accused Darden of "State U-ism." Although the University of Virginia is a state university, it is also the premier institution in a state with no comparable private university. In a sense, it has tried to fulfill both roles. Students and alumni of the 1950s wanted to distinguish the University of Virginia from midwestern state universities, which they saw as sprawling, impersonal degree factories. Fraternity members argued that under Darden's lead, the university was exerting too much control over student life, by limiting the hours during which women could visit the fraternity houses, requiring a female chaperone at every fraternity party, tracking academic records of all fraternity members, and overseeing fraternity finances.

At the center of the controversy over the changing university stood Newcomb Hall, the student activities center, which opened in 1958. With a cafeteria and a snack bar, lounges, meeting rooms, a ballroom, game rooms, a post office, and even a bowling alley, it was to be a "hangout," a place for students to go "to be with the crowd," one professor said; but not all students saw it that way. Many regarded it as a symbol of the university's efforts to centralize and to control student life. While the alumni magazine quoted one student as saying, "I don't know how we've gotten along without it," others mocked the building, calling it "Ping Pong Palace" and the "Stupid Union Building."

Newcomb Hall. *Before it opened, students saw the new student activities building as a symbol of President Darden's efforts to centralize and control the university's social life. Opposition died as soon as the building opened in 1958.*

First African American student, Gregory Swanson.

Already a practicing lawyer, Swanson won admission to graduate study in law through a court decree requiring the university to admit qualified African American applicants when black colleges did not provide comparable educational offerings. Swanson remained at the law school for less than a year, returning to the practice of law in the spring of 1951. Above, the Carver Inn on Preston Avenue, the one African American hotel near the university in the 1950s.

Tradition's Shifting Ground

In 1950, Gregory Hayes Swanson applied for admission to graduate study in law at the university. He was already an attorney, practicing law in Danville with a degree from Howard University. Supported by the NAACP and represented by, among others, Thurgood Marshall, Swanson was challenging the institution and the state. With his credentials, had he been white he would have been admitted to the University of Virginia.

Swanson was not the first African American to apply to the university. In 1935 Alice Jackson, a Richmond woman who had already studied French at Smith College, requested admission to graduate study. The Board of Visitors directed John C. Metcalf, the dean of graduate studies, to "refuse respectfully the pending application of a colored student," since "the admission of white and colored persons in the same schools is contrary to the long established and fixed policy of the Commonwealth." From that date into the 1940s, the Commonwealth of Virginia funded a program, similar to those already in place in Missouri, West Virginia, and Maryland, that paid black students' tuition at schools in northern states like Ohio, New York, and Michigan. Jackson accepted $75 and a round-trip train ticket to Columbia University. In 1986 Alice Jackson Stuart retired after a full career of college teaching.

When Gregory Swanson applied, the university referred again to the principle of school segregation with which they had denied Alice Jackson admission. Swanson brought suit against the university, and a federal appeals court found denying him admission an infringement of his Fourteenth Amendment rights. He entered the university in September 1950 but returned to his law practice before the end of the academic year.

Gregory Swanson's action opened the door for African Americans to attend the University of Virginia. In his 1951 annual report, Colgate Darden mentioned that "several Negroes" had enrolled in the university's graduate and professional degree programs. One such student was Walter N. Ridley, who enrolled in the school of education and in 1953 became not only the first African American to receive a degree from the University of Virginia

but also the first African American to receive a doctoral degree from any southern white institution. In 1953 Edward B. Nash and Edward T. Wood, both African American students from Richmond, entered the medical school.

As the first few black students entered graduate and professional schools in the early 1950s, about two hundred women enrolled annually as well. Most were in nursing, education, and graduate school, a few in law or medicine. Even fewer were undergraduates in the College of Arts and Sciences, which did not yet admit women for a full four-year course of study. Some third-year transfers were accepted from Mary Washington, the university's coordinate women's college until 1972. Women entered as first-year education majors, and in fact some claimed that they were using the education school as a "back door" into the College of Arts and Sciences. Edward J. McShane, chairman of mathematics, refused an offer from the University of Minnesota, on the condition that his daughters be allowed to attend the University of Virginia. Eventually, faculty daughters, faculty wives, and Charlottesville girls who lived at home received permission to enter the College, so arts and sciences classes of the 1950s often had one or two women in attendance.

Jesse W. Beams, renowned physicist. *Jesse Beams conducted significant physics experiments at the university from 1928 to his retirement in 1969 and after, working into the mid-1970s with other university scientists in pursuit of an ever-more accurate measurement of the gravitational constant. Here, Beams (right) and the chemistry professor Allan Gwathmey observe the ultracentrifuge Beams developed.*

The Atomic Age

On 4 October 1957, the Soviet Union launched Sputnik, the first satellite to orbit earth. By 6 November 1957, a dog was circling earth in Sputnik II. "Our general missile program is bringing up the rear in this race," the *Cavalier Daily* commented. "The Soviet scientists have achieved a nicety of measurement that we can only dream about and it is to be hoped that our program will get the shot in the arm that it needs with a minimum of delay. If it does not, we may soon have a lot more to worry about than the fate of a lonely little dog which is now circling the earth at a speed unknown to man."

The success of Sputnik made many American educators question their programs in mathematics and science. Lawrence R. Quarles, an alumnus and physicist, worked to refocus the engineering program, which had since the turn of the century trained students in practical technologies such as power generation and industrial chemistry. Named dean in 1955, Quarles emphasized the science underlying engineering applications, an influence signaled in the new name: the School of Engineering and Applied Science.

In the College of Arts and Sciences, physics, chemistry, and biology received a boost, thanks to donations from John Lee Pratt. A General Motors executive involved in the development of the refrigerant Freon, Pratt had studied engineering at the University of Virginia. He donated a GM motor to the engineering school but found, on a visit to his alma mater, that it had been neglected. Some say he found the motor still in its shipping crate, others say it had been left out in the rain, but whatever the story, Pratt's generosity toward engineering ceased. Including the bequest that came at his death in 1975, Pratt contributed twelve million dollars to the university—none of which went to engineering. His endowment continues to bolster laboratory research and student fellowships in the basic sciences.

Virginia's greatest scientific accomplishments during the 1950s occurred in the laboratory of Jesse W. Beams, who had conducted groundbreaking work in physics since the 1930s, when Beams developed a small centrifuge motor that revolved 1.2 million times per minute and generated a centrifugal force 300,000 times the force of gravity. By the time he retired, Beams's centrifuges had reached the speed of 1.5 million rotations per minute and a force 1 billion times that of gravity.

"His entire interest was in physics," recalls Frank L. Hereford, who studied and then taught with Beams. "He expected everyone to be there all the time. Weekends didn't amount to anything in his mind." During the war, experiments in Beams's lab would run twenty hours straight. W. Dexter Whitehead, another student-turned-colleague of Beams's, describes working on a "rock and roll table" designed to simulate the pitch and yaw of an aircraft carrier, to test centrifuge-based guided missiles. During the war years armed guards stood outside the physics laboratory as Beams trained his ultracentrifuge on the top-secret task of separating uranium isotopes, an alternative

Early electron microscopy, ca. 1960. *Engineering professor Kenneth Lawless examines the atomic structure of materials through one of the university's first electron microscopes.*

High-voltage experimentation. *Three physics graduate students, working in 1946, adjust a Mark circuit, designed to produce high voltages for research effects. The student at center, Robert Kuhlthau, became a professor of engineering. The student at right, Frank L. Hereford Jr., became a professor of physics and the university's fifth president.*

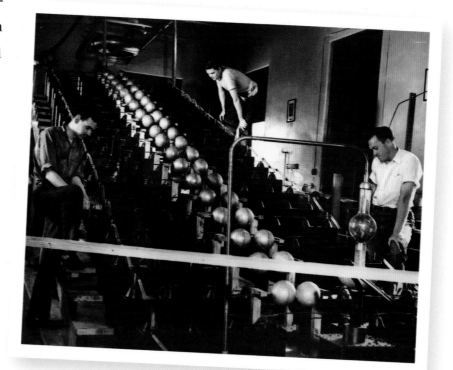

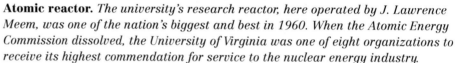

Atomic reactor. *The university's research reactor, here operated by J. Lawrence Meem, was one of the nation's biggest and best in 1960. When the Atomic Energy Commission dissolved, the University of Virginia was one of eight organizations to receive its highest commendation for service to the nuclear energy industry.*

Beloved mutt. *Found in front of Alderman Library by a commerce school student named Buzz Speakman, Seal became part of university life, even traveling with football fans to games such as that against the University of Pennsylvania in 1949. Like Beta, the dog who came before him, Seal was mourned in grandiose style when he died in 1953, a cortege bearing his body to the cemetery.*

method to gaseous diffusion, ultimately used for the bomb produced by the Manhattan Project. Beams's centrifuge technique received renewed attention when Jimmy Carter advocated it for atomic energy generation in 1977.

Beams's presence made Virginia a prime candidate for postwar research in atomic energy. During the late 1950s the university received over a million dollars from the Atomic Energy Commission, and in 1960 its million-watt swimming-pool-type nuclear reactor went into operation. "It is the most powerful in the South and as versatile as any in the nation for teaching and research," engineering dean Quarles stated. Students trained to operate nuclear power plants. Faculty used the reactor for basic research in atomic physics and applied research on trace elements in the environment, on cancer therapies, and on semiconductor manufacturing. As the nuclear power industry dwindled, however, the rationale for such a facility at the university weakened, and in 1998 the reactor closed.

The Library Advances

During the 1950s the University of Virginia Library continued to build its collections. Just after World War II archivist Francis L. Berkeley Jr., driving a brand-new Chrysler thanks to an alumnus, traveled the state to call on families who might own papers and letters relating to Virginia history.

On the Rotunda steps. *For all generations of University of Virginia students, the broad span of steps leading from the Rotunda's south portal down to the Lawn has been a favorite resting spot.*

The women of Mary Washington. *In 1955 Mademoiselle magazine visited the University of Virginia, asking female students enrolled in Mary Washington, then the university's coordinate women's college, to model sports and evening wear in picturesque settings around the grounds.*

"The war had turned things upside down, and country people were moving to the city," says Berkeley. "I knew there was a great richness of family papers and manuscripts in Virginia, and so I visited descendants of politicians and so forth. They considered it a great compliment that the university wanted their papers." Not only did Berkeley acquire manuscripts

C. Waller Barrett, literary benefactor. *From the late 1940s on, book collector and alumnus Clifton Waller Barrett contributed first editions and manuscripts to the university, ultimately representing the fullest body of American literature ever collected. The Barrett Reading Room opened in Alderman Library in 1960. Here Barrett displays manuscripts of Washington Irving's* Sketch-book *and Stephen Crane's* Red Badge of Courage.

representing the great families of Virginia—Randolph, Cabell, Glass—but he also developed a strong collection of literary papers from authors including Ellen Glasgow and John Dos Passos.

Between 1945 and 1948, the university's special collections more than doubled in size to over three million books, manuscripts, letters, and documents. A million manuscripts were acquired in 1947–48 alone. That year's acquisitions ranged from manuscripts of eighteenth-century chamber music and early maps of Kentucky to prints of modern French art. By 1955, the university librarian Harry Clemons reported that library holdings numbered over five million, representing growth one hundred–fold in fifty years.

Clemons's 1948 report briefly mentions a few American first editions donated by alumnus Clifton Waller Barrett, who for the next forty years would remain a central figure in the building of the library's special collections. Barrett graduated from the university in 1920 and, beginning as a clerk, built a shipping empire through the 1930s and 1940s. He retired in 1954 and directed his energy toward his real love, collecting books. "I wrote James Southall Wilson, who had been a professor of mine at the university," Barrett said in 1986. "He told me no institution or individual had ever extensively collected American literature, and that I should try that."

Barrett spent fifty years building the world's most complete collection of American manuscripts and first editions, making it clear from early on that he was collecting in partnership with the university. He hosted Robert Frost at the 1960 ceremonial opening of Alderman Library's Barrett Room, designed to house his collection of over 250,000 items, valued then at three million dollars. Barrett continued collecting until his death in 1991. Highlights of his collection include the letters and manuscripts of Charles Brockden Brown, the first American novelist; Walt Whitman's letters, notebooks, and manuscripts leading up to *Leaves of Grass;* the copy of *A Week on the Concord and Merrimack Rivers* that Thoreau presented to Tennyson, as well as the map he and his brother used during that expedition; and a Vachel Lindsay archive, with published and unpublished poems as well as his literary papers. University librarians estimate the value of the Barrett Collection today at more than fifty million dollars.

Jefferson Biographer

On 13 April 1948, Dumas Malone (left) presented to President Darden a copy of the first volume of his biography of Thomas Jefferson. Published that very day, Jefferson the Virginian *was dedicated to the University of Virginia. Malone had taught briefly at Virginia in the 1920s, and he returned in 1959, becoming the university's biographer-in-residence. In 1975, he received the Pulitzer Prize in history for his ongoing biography of Jefferson, the sixth and final volume of which he completed at the age of eighty-nine.*

Mr. Faulkner's Visits

A number of writers visited the university from the late 1940s on, some briefly, like Robert Frost, others for a week, a semester, or longer. "Thank God Katherine Anne Porter was writer-in-residence when I was there," says author Richard Dillard, a professor of creative writing at Hollins University and a student at Virginia from 1958 to 1964. "I would take her my stories and she would read them out loud to me. I would hear everything that was wrong. It made me squirm. She would talk about them as she read. She was so kind to me." The humorist Peter de Vries, the poet Stephen Spender, and the historian Shelby Foote also visited the university.

No visiting writer left as lasting an impression, however, as did William Faulkner, writer-in-residence during the springs of 1957 and 1958, then a lecturer starting in 1959. "He was one of the most important things that happened to me," says Douglas Day, author and professor at the university today, a graduate student when Faulkner was on the grounds. "He was the lord. He was the man. He had just won the Nobel Prize. The faculty more or less helped him in his desire for privacy, and I think we didn't pay him enough attention, we were so careful. He probably spent a lonely time here."

Those who knew him always mention his natty dress. "Harris tweed breeches, cordovan shoes. The epitome of male fashion. Faulkner had it all down," says Day. "He was faintly shabby, but clean and stylish,

William Faulkner, reluctant lecturer. *Twice in residence at the university during the late 1950s, Faulkner spoke before a variety of classes and clubs. He found other ways to engage in the life of students as well, including serving as timekeeper for the track team.*

and he always wore this silly little porkpie hat. He wanted to look like an English lord." He became a member of both Keswick and Farmington country clubs, joining equestrian society, and had his portrait painted in his fox-hunting pink.

"He was this dapper little guy who would turn up here and there," remembers the Pulitzer Prize–winning poet Henry Taylor, an undergraduate while Faulkner was at the university. Faulkner met an occasional class but often acted as if he had little to say. "He would begin by saying something like, 'I see quite a few students here today, and I am aware that they have been reading *Light in August,*'" says Taylor. "He would put his fingertips together and look around. He would just stand there. Fifteen seconds, thirty seconds. He wasn't going to say anything until he got a question. He would stand there all day. So some poor bastard would finally have to ask him something, like, 'Mr. Faulkner, what's your philosophy of life?' He would answer, 'Fear God, women, and the police.' The end. That was the answer to that question."

Henry Taylor remembers how refreshing he found it to meet a great author who could talk conversationally about art. "He would talk about *The Sound and the Fury* the way you could talk about buying a car. He wrote this book, and he was a guy. He wasn't superhuman." From Faulkner, Taylor learned that "you can take your art as seriously as you want, but be careful about taking yourself seriously."

THE PROFESSIONAL SCHOOLS

As professional education developed in the United States, separate schools evolved at the university, including the School of Medicine, the School of Law, the McIntire School of Commerce, and the Darden Graduate School of Business Education.

phitheater, which he described as an "almost perpendicular two-story theater."

Dr. Paul B. Barringer, on the faculty from 1888 to 1907, recognized that a practicing and research hospital was essential to a successful medical school. Foundations were dug, but a lack of funds kept the university from building a hospital for several years, and the site

Medicine

The earliest medical students attended lectures and demonstrations on physiology and surgery in the Anatomical Theater, a small building that used to stand west of the Lawn. After each lecture students observed the dispensary clinic, during which the professor offered medical and surgical assistance to local citizens, who paid up to fifty cents per consultation.

In 1838, under the professor of anatomy James L. Cabell, students began performing their own dissections. They paid a $3.50 annual dissecting fee and worked on cats, dogs, and cadavers, when available, and only in cold weather. A janitor, whom students called "Anatomical Lewis," cleaned the surgical instruments and, once the study was complete, boiled the remains and salvaged the bones for anatomy classes. Students also observed actual surgeries performed by faculty members. One medical alumnus remembered witnessing his first operation, a thyroidectomy, in 1916, in the surgical am-

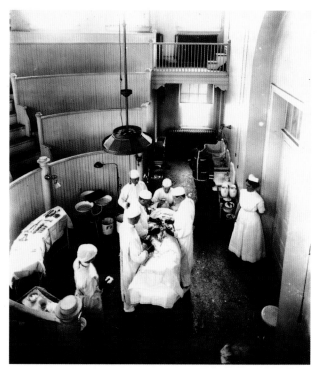

Top: Paul Barringer, professor of medicine and hospital founder. Above: Surgery demonstrations, ca. 1910.

University Hospital, ca. 1990

was dubbed "Barringer's Frog Pond." The first hospital wing opened in 1901. President Alderman waged a fierce battle in the early 1920s, when legislators threatened to move the medical school to Richmond, where, they contended, a larger population needed medical care. Once the legislature agreed that the school should stay in Charlottesville, new hospital and medical school buildings were erected, including the Davis wing, dedicated to mental treatment, named after John Staige Davis, who had taught the university's first neurology course in 1908.

As the hospital served more patients, it needed more staff. The university's first course for nurses started in 1901, essentially an apprenticeship that guaranteed workers in the hospital and in the field. "The hospital would be called upon for nurses by the harassed country doctor," recalled Florence Besley, nursing superintendent from 1901 to 1907. "These girls took charge in mountain cabins with no sanitary facilities, no help, . . . and with a doctor or an outsider a rare sight."

Even when the university established an academically oriented nursing program within the education school in the 1920s, the hospital continued to train licensed practical nurses. In 1950 a third nursing program was established, under the aegis of the School of Medicine. Finally, in 1953, nursing education coalesced into a single department, soon designated the School of Nursing.

A major hospital addition in 1960 almost doubled medical care facilities. In 1989 a new University Hospital opened, with 552 beds, 19 operating rooms, and 7 intensive care units, "a model for the nation and the envy of its peers," according to Dr. Louis P. Sullivan, U.S. secretary of health and human services. In the academic year 1996–97, 485,000 outpatients received care at university medical facilities.

As the pace of medical research intensified around the world, the university built extensive new facilities, including, by the mid-1970s, the seven-story Jordan Hall, which housed research laboratories exclusively, and a new health sciences library. Ongoing work in Virginia laboratories in the late twentieth century held far-reaching promise, as researchers sought, for example, a contraceptive vaccine and genetic indicators for Alzheimer's and Parkinson's diseases.

Law

In early days, law study was offered to all students at the University of Virginia. The Junior courses concentrated on principles—the laws of nature and nations, the constitution, the theory of government—while senior courses focused on practice—common, statute, maritime, and commercial law.

For fifty years, from 1845 to 1895, John B. Minor embodied the study of law at Virginia, where he himself had studied math, chemistry, ancient and modern languages, and civil engineering, as well as both levels of law. Minor could "cut the law into thin slices," Senator John W. Daniels, a law alumnus, recalled, and "cater it out in forms

John B. Minor, professor of law. Below: School of Law, 1997.

of appetizing delicacy and easy digestion." Minor established a moot court, which he called "a precise counterpart of the several tribunals" of Virginia, and he required all law students to participate. He gave written examinations at a time when other law professors examined their students orally.

Minor also believed in teaching rules, reasoning, and theory at a time when other law schools were discovering the case-study method. "We find ourselves almost in a class to ourselves," wrote law dean William M. Lile in the 1920s, "thought of, and not infrequently referred to by our contemporaries, as old-fogyish and out of date. But we have held to our own methods—not from ignorance of the virtues of the other system, but from deliberate choice." After Armistead Dobie became dean in 1932, the case method of studying law came into use at Virginia.

In the early twentieth century, law professors

Morrison Law Library, 1997

jealously watched from their classrooms in the basement wing of the Rotunda as medicine and engineering departments gained their own buildings. They complained, calling the law department "the only fowl in the poultry yard of the University that lays golden eggs." Fully one-third of all students at that time were enrolled in law. In 1911 Minor Hall opened for law classes, but soon it was outgrown. In 1932 Clark Hall opened, with a larger library and a magisterial lobby ornamented with larger-than-life figures depicting the history of the law.

Dean of law from 1939 to 1963, F. D. G. Ribble epitomized the Socratic method of teaching. "Some thought he pushed it to an extreme by his apparent unwillingness to express his own views," wrote Hardy C. Dillard, Ribble's successor, in a 1971 reminiscence. Throughout the tense years of integration, both in Virginia's public schools and at the university, President Colgate Darden relied on Ribble for legal advice.

By the middle of the twentieth century, the University of Virginia law school was considered among

the nation's finest. *The Kiplinger Report* ranked Virginia among the nation's top seven law schools in 1960. "It is in the South that the Virginia Law School is least recognized," read an article in the *University of Virginia Magazine*. Virginians accounted for only 30 percent of law students, and the "exodus north" of many graduates built the law school's reputation more solidly in that direction.

Law students influenced the entire university through the Student Legal Forum, founded in 1948

Edward, John, and (law alumnus) Robert Kennedy at the university, 1958

by, among others, Robert F. Kennedy, a 1951 graduate. Each year the Student Legal Forum sponsored addresses by relevant public figures. In the 1972–73 school year, for example, a time of heated political debate, the forum brought twenty-five speakers, from Senator Hubert Humphrey and Congresswoman Shirley Chisholm to Admiral Elmo Zumwalt and Vice President Spiro Agnew.

With its own weekly newspaper, student council, and prestigious student-edited law review, the law school of the 1970s represented a culture all of its own. The law library holdings totaled 150,000, including a distinguished collection in international law. These factors made the move in 1975 to a new building on the North Grounds all the more natural. In 1997 expansion and renovation of the David A. Harrison III Law Grounds were completed.

The university's first undergraduate degrees in commerce, granted in 1921, went to students enrolled in the Wilson School of Economics, named after James Wilson, a signer of the Declaration of Independence. That very year, Charlottesville philanthropist Paul Goodloe McIntire donated $200,000 for undergraduate business studies. For decades the McIntire School of Commerce existed side by side with the School of Economics, both part of the College of Arts and Sciences, with the economics professor Tipton R. Snavely serving as faculty liaison between the two groups.

Snavely began discussing Virginia's need for a graduate school of business management as early as

Tipton Snavely. Below: new Darden School building.

1946. Students could study commerce as undergraduates, but for the M.B.A. they went to Harvard, Stanford, or Columbia Universities. In March 1948 President Darden presented the idea to the Virginia Industry Management Conference, and support for a Virginia M.B.A. program began to gain momentum.

"No exclusively graduate business school existed in the South in 1954, or indeed in a state university anywhere," wrote Charles C. Abbott, who came from Harvard as dean of the new school. A graduate business school would keep the "mental topsoil" at home in Virginia and in the south, as the Richmond banker and early supporter J. Harvie Wilkinson Jr. put it. The school started off with a bang—literally. As Abbott greeted the entering class, the marketing professor Everard Meade, a Madison Avenue man who once wrote for Jack Benny, shot off a cannon outside Monroe Hall.

Darden's support of the school was commemorated when it took his name in 1974, becoming the

Darden School of Graduate Business Administration. The Darden School program led to the M.B.A., while the McIntire School accepted third-year students seeking a B.S. in commerce and graduate students seeking master's degrees in specialized business fields.

In 1975 the Darden School moved into a new building on the North Grounds, and Monroe Hall was rededicated for the McIntire School of Commerce. In 1987 the Balfour Addition doubled commerce school facilities in a building praised for its neoclassic elegance. Architecture professor Richard Guy Wilson commented that "you don't even know it is new, it is so good."

Faculties at both schools followed the case method of teaching, brought by Abbott from Harvard. Mirroring the business world, Darden and McIntire School professors often structured assignments as team projects, like the legendary financial forecasting and strategy project undertaken by all commerce school finance majors. Teams of four to

six students were asked to forecast the upcoming gross domestic product and to interpret its effect on a specific industry and company.

Both schools capitalized on lively connections with the business community. As early as the 1930s, commerce faculty were working with the banking industry, a partnership that developed into a national, then an international, banking school run by the McIntire School. From 1986 students at the McIntire School ran an executive-in-residence program, inviting business leaders to meet and teach them.

A steering committee of Virginia business leaders drove early Darden School efforts in the 1950s, winning the allegiance of numerous sponsors, nicknamed "Charlie Abbott's Instant Alumni." The school's first executive program was offered in November 1955, a short course entitled "Working Capital." By 1998 Darden's executive programs had grown tremendously, drawing four thousand mid-level and top managers to Charlottesville for courses each year.

A Time of Change

Edgar F. Shannon, fourth president of the university

Faculty were surprised when, after Colgate Darden's retirement from the presidency in 1959, Edgar F. Shannon was selected to be the fourth president of the University of Virginia. A newcomer to the university—hired as associate professor of English three years before—forty-one-year-old Shannon was still one of their own. Although a "mink" (from Washington and Lee), he had impeccable credentials, with degrees from Harvard, Duke, and Oxford, where he had been a Rhodes scholar. "He was thoroughly academic," says Francis L. Berkeley Jr. Whereas Colgate Darden took pride when other universities recruited from his faculty, Shannon recognized the danger of such a "brain drain" and turned the flow around.

From 1960 to 1970, the university faculty grew in number from 461 to 1,121. Undergraduate enrollment more than doubled; graduate enrollments tripled. The National Science Foundation and the National Institutes of Health granted significant new sums in federal funding. The National Defense Education Act provided loans and fellowships with which to attract more and better graduate students. Virginia's research programs grew stronger, with sponsored research revenues up from three million dollars in 1960 to sixteen million ten years later.

1970

- *10,850 students*

- *950 faculty members*

- *821 staff members*

- *Tuition: $330 for Virginians; $915 for non-Virginians*

- *Lawn rooms: $310 per year*

- *Estimated annual undergraduate expenses: $1,085–$1,355, including $125–$175 for books*

Registration in Mem Gym. *As the university grew larger, registration for classes—staged for years in Memorial Gymnasium—became more complex.*

Education, according to Shannon, was one of the weapons with which the Cold War would be won. "The Soviet Union has embraced education as a tool for self-aggrandizement," Edgar Shannon said in his inaugural address in 1959. "The nations of the West cannot refuse the gauntlet.... Manpower and willpower are integral, but brainpower is crucial to survival."

Creative to Spite Tradition

A new publication appeared on the university grounds in 1960. Called *Plume and Sword,* it considered its job "to honor the honorable and to ridicule the ridiculous." For six years *Plume and Sword* influenced university aesthetics and politics, publishing the early writings of many destined for literary acclaim. The poets Henry Taylor and Kelly Cherry, the fiction writer and literary critic Richard Dillard—all three University of Virginia students at this time—contributed to *Plume and Sword,* as did students from nearby Hollins College, notably the novelist Lee Smith and the essayist Annie Dillard, who wrote under her maiden name, Annie Doak. English professor Fred Bornhauser, hired to teach literature, invited students to meet weekly at his home and share their writing. They nicknamed the sessions their "bootleg poetry seminar." "I don't think many schools had the kind of artistic energy that bubbled up here at that time," says George Garrett, who taught creative writing at the university then and later. "There's never been anything like it again."

For Henry Taylor, it was a time of "weird arrogance." Richard Dillard remembers playing whiffle ball inside New Cabell Hall, the ball careening from the English department to "the other end of this interminably long hall, where math department faculty members sat brooding over equations." "We had crazies all the time," recalls John T. Casteen, a graduate student in those days, later to become the university's president. In 1961, Casteen points out, Gus Hall (general secretary of the American

Upstart literary magazine. Plume and Sword *began as a typed and mimeographed collection of poems and opinion pieces written by a small group of students. It developed over the next eight years into an attractive literary journal. Editor Stephen Barney even succeeded in acquiring an unpublished poem from E. E. Cummings.*

Communist Party) and George Lincoln Rockwell (head of the American Nazi Party) both spoke at the university.

Bob Dylan would be seen on the Corner or riding a bike across the Lawn. Josh White, Joan Baez, and Peter, Paul, and Mary sang in Old Cabell Hall, as did Charlottesville's own Slithy Toves, with a psychedelic light show "guaranteed to blow your mind." To draw attention to writer Shelby Foote's McGregor Room reading, a Dixieland band strutted through the library stacks. Students climbed up onto the roof of the Rotunda one dawn in 1965 and left behind a 250-pound calf. Only thirty years later, at his 1996 class reunion, did Alfred R. Berkeley III—a student council officer then, now president of NASDAQ—admit to the crime.

The New Face of Student Politics

In the 1950s candidates had run for student council as members of Lambda Pi or Skull and Keys, the two political parties, but there was no conflict over issues. Alexander G. Gilliam, a student from 1951 to 1954 who later became secretary to the Board of Visitors, remembers campaigning with a fraternity brother door to door and being asked about their party platform. "We just looked at each other," says Gilliam. "We didn't have an answer."

Joan Baez sings. *Folk music laced with protest messages marked the times. In 1965 Joan Baez sang for students during the Beaux Arts Ball.*

March down the Lawn. *During the late 1960s and early 1970s, frequent protests over national and local issues turned academic processions into political demonstrations on Jefferson's Lawn.*

In the 1960s, student election platforms called for change at the university and in people's consciousness. For the first time, students elected "independents"—candidates from outside the fraternity-controlled political system—to the student council. In 1968 more students voted than anyone could remember having voted before, and Anarchist Party candidates swept the election. A chapter of Students for a Democratic Society formed, and amid much debate the student council granted them one hundred dollars from its activities budget. In 1969 students elected James Roebuck president of the student council—an independent, a graduate student, and an African American.

In May 1970, days after Nixon announced the invasion of Cambodia, National Guardsmen shot and killed four youths at Kent State University. Students at Princeton called for a nationwide strike. At Virginia, students confronted President Shannon with demands that included removing the

Homer goes on strike. *At the University of Virginia, as at colleges and universities across the nation, Nixon's decision to bomb Cambodia and the killings at Kent State brought about strikes, protests, sit-ins, and rallies.*

ROTC from university grounds and committing to a goal of 20 percent black enrollment. Students occupied Naval ROTC offices in Maury Hall and rallied on the steps of the Rotunda, but the protest was "near death," according to the *Cavalier Daily,* until the radical lawyer William Kunstler and the yippie leader Jerry Rubin rekindled fires.

Kunstler and Rubin, on tour through the nation's campuses, had been scheduled to come to the University of Virginia for weeks. Officials considered canceling the event, but they feared cancellation would provoke a worse reaction. As thousands of young people filled University Hall, state police moved in on Charlottesville, ready for confrontation. Kunstler energized the audience with a call to shut down the university. Someone grabbed the microphone and cried out, "On to Carr's Hill!" Crowds poured out the doors, and as many as two thousand stampeded the president's house. Kunstler joined marchers on the president's porch, exhorting them to action. Shannon, meeting with Roebuck and other students, chose to stay inside. "I and some others said, trying to divert them, 'Let's go burn Maury Hall'—something like that," recalled Whittington Clement, president of the College of Arts and Sciences and honor committee chair, a few years later. The

Up against the wall. *University of Virginia demonstrators wore coats and ties and created their own genteel versions of protest slogans.*

As a point of information and clarification we are not running as a joke. We selected the title Anarchist because we intend to destroy the present style of student government.... We adopted a light-hearted style of campaigning to relieve the men of the College of the infinite boredom of the regular "honky" campaign.

— Walker Lawrence Chandler and Charles Andrew Murdock, Anarchist candidates for student council, 1968

177

War protesters at Jefferson's feet. *In October 1969, university students gathered outside the Rotunda to protest American actions in the Vietnam War.*

crowd surged toward the NROTC building, where a smoldering mattress, which had been lit deliberately in the basement, deterred them.

On Friday, 8 May 1970—a day on which strikes and demonstrations shut down 224 colleges across the country—protesters blocked traffic on University Avenue, holding up signs with such slogans as "Honk for Peace." Fraternity brothers, not much involved in antiwar politics, were escorting dates that evening to a black-tie event in the Rotunda. Whit Clement remembered that as he and his date stepped outside, "all of a sudden the cops were coming up the hill with their billy sticks and we all started running." No one believed that police would raid the Lawn. "I got in my room on the Lawn," said Clement. "About thirty people came in the room with me.... The cops were pulling people out by their ankles ... It was absolutely unforgettable." Police rounded up protestors, party-goers, and student marshals alike in a Mayflower van. Sixty-eight were arrested in all, including an editor of the *Cavalier Daily,* a university groundskeeper, a pizza delivery man, and a Georgia lawyer visiting his son. That night's police action "did more than anything else to radicalize student opinion," said James Roebuck. The next day, twenty-nine fraternities signed their support for the student strike.

On 10 May, President Shannon addressed a crowd of four thousand from the south portico of the Rotunda. "As we meet here this afternoon, the University of Virginia is the only major university on the East Coast that is really open," he began. "I intend to keep it open." Some responded with boos and hisses, but Shannon continued. "Never before have I been more proud of the students and faculty of the University than I am today.... All of our students are deeply concerned about the war, some to the point where in an agony of conscience they want to act, not to study." He urged faculty to allow extensions so students could "concentrate on constructive action

James Roebuck reads student demands. *During the tumultuous nights of early May 1970, student protesters faced administrators and police in the streets. Here, the student council president James Roebuck (right) reads student demands before crowds of protesters as President Shannon (left) and Professor D. Alan Williams (center) look on. Roebuck was later elected to the Pennsylvania legislature.*

May Days, 1970. *In part memory book, in part political statement, this booklet was created by Rob Buford, Peter Shea, and Andy Stickney, three Cavalier Daily editors, to chronicle events at the University of Virginia during the intense week when college students across the United States demonstrated in anger against the invasion of Cambodia and the killing of protesters at Kent State.*

Larry Sabato, national pundit.
Student council president in 1973, Sabato returned to the University of Virginia in 1978 as professor of government and foreign affairs and became a media commentator in high demand on state and national politics in the 1980s and 1990s.

in the re-direction of the nation's war policy." He read a statement to Virginia's Senators Spong and Byrd decrying the "anti-intellectualism and growing militarism" of the U.S. government. Shannon's speech, wrote the *Cavalier Daily,* was "a rallying point for all of us."

"The University Bows," accused the *Richmond Times-Dispatch* the next morning: "Shannon looks very much like a man who is prepared to back down." Governor Linwood Holton denounced Shannon's stand, and letters to the editor poured in to the *Times-Dispatch,* some calling for Shannon's dismissal. One month later, at the final exercises on 7 June 1970, however, Edgar Shannon received a standing ovation. Alumni correspondence was piling up in his office, three to one against his stand, yet he insisted that "there are times when personal neutrality—and failure to express convictions on issues gripping the nation and the university community—can be fatal."

Political consciousness continued to characterize the leadership and activities of the student council even after war protests had peaked. Students called for increased minority representation at the university, for full rights for gay students, and for improved pay and work conditions for service staff. They also began pressing for student representation on the Board of Visitors. It was in this arena that Larry Sabato first gained a voice in politics, being elected as vice president and then as president of the student council in his student years. Sabato graduated in 1974 and attended Oxford as a Rhodes scholar before returning to the University of Virginia faculty and becoming a nationally recognized political commentator. During election season Sabato found himself fielding several dozen phone calls daily from newspaper editors and radio and television producers asking for his analysis and prediction. "I live it, I breathe it," said Sabato in 1997 of electoral politics. He coined the motto, well known to his students, "Politics is a good thing." His two books *Feeding Frenzy: How Attack Journalism Has Transformed American Politics* (1993) and *Dirty Little Secrets: The Persistence of Corruption in American Politics* (1996) analyzed key trends in contemporary politics.

Coats and ties disappearing.
*The university had imposed no
dress code since the 1830s, but
up until 1970, University of
Virginia students chose to wear
coats and ties to class. In the
late 1960s, the tradition weakened. Bradley H. Gunter, a
graduate student and English
instructor in the mid-1960s,
remembers coats and ties above,
shorts or sweatpants below.
"And nobody ever wore socks,"
says Gunter. "Bare feet and
Weejuns."*

Wesley Harris, first African American student to live on the Lawn. *Advised by his high school teacher to choose engineering over physics, since none of Virginia's black colleges offered engineering at the time, Harris entered the university in 1960, winning significant honors, including a room on the Lawn. Harris later became a professor of aeronautics and astronautics at M.I.T.*

A quarter century later. *By 1997, when brothers Tiki and Ronde Barber graduated from the commerce school (below), the proportion of black students attending the university had grown to 9 percent.*

Opening the Doors

Political activism was both the effect and cause of a changing student body at the University of Virginia. Faculty members who had fought for school desegregation in Charlottesville turned their fervor back to the university. Even into the 1960s, only a small number of African American undergraduates entered the university, first through the engineering school. "The law was that Virginia had to provide educational opportunities to blacks that were comparable to those offered to whites," explains O. Allan Gianniny, a young engineering faculty member in those days. "There were colleges of arts and sciences for blacks, so the university was not required to admit students to the college. On the other hand, there was no black engineering school in Virginia."

"I wanted to earn a college degree in physics," says Wesley L. Harris. As a student at Richmond's all-black Armstrong High School, Harris had studied physics with Eloise Bowles Washington, an African American woman with a master's degree in physics from the University of Pennsylvania. Bowles encouraged Harris to go into engineering instead, because that way he could attend the University of Virginia.

Now a professor of aeronautics at M.I.T., Harris entered the University of Virginia in 1960. On his first day at the university, his white roommate moved out, refusing to share a room with him. Student health nurses seemed afraid to touch him. A calculus professor made comments in class implying that Harris might never learn mathematics. There were five other African American students in engineering, older than himself, whom he soon befriended. They told him that the University Cafeteria was the only Corner restaurant that would serve them. Together, they went downtown for church services and Sunday dinner, feeling more at home in Charlottesville's black community than they did at the university. "We were somewhat considered heroes, and so we were welcomed," says Harris.

Some white professors genuinely supported and encouraged him, says Harris, but through all four years he never saw a black professor, a black administrator, or a female professor. Black students joined white faculty and community members to work for integration, boycotting restaurants, picketing movie theaters, and convincing barbers to open their businesses to customers of every color. Elected into the Jefferson Society and the engineering honor society, Harris ultimately won the privilege of living on the Lawn—the first African American student to be awarded these honors. Harris is proud of his achievements, but he also points out that not all African Americans who broke the color barrier at white institutions survived as well as he did.

Stepping with pride. *While black fraternities and sororities were established nationally by 1920, it was not until the mid-1970s that local chapters were established at the University of Virginia. Here, Phi Beta Sigma brothers perform a step show, ca. 1985.*

"There was a lot of anger among the six or seven of us, but we expressed it in different ways," Harris says. "Rather than write letters to the editor, we decided to pass physics with an A. That nobody can take away from you. If you had pent-up emotions, the academic route was the best way to express those emotions." Harris went on to earn a Ph.D. at Princeton, where he found even fewer black classmates than at Virginia.

On 11 April 1968, one week after the assassination of Martin Luther King Jr., Roy Wilkins, the executive director of the NAACP, addressed a university audience so large that the event was moved from a classroom building to the athletic arena. Throughout the nation, believes M. Rick Turner, dean of African American affairs at the university since 1988, King's death marked a turning point in the educational options open to African Americans. In 1969 the university hired its first black admissions officer. That year, among about ten thousand students, 134 were African Americans.

Sylvia Terry, an assistant dean of African American studies at the university, entered the graduate department of English in 1971. "I was one of one or two black students in class," she recalls. "When I saw another black woman on the sidewalk, I ran up and introduced myself. The community was so small that we did support one another."

Women Enter the College

In 1969 a young Charlottesville woman named Virginia Anne Scott went to work for John Lowe, a 1967 Virginia law school graduate dedicated to defending difficult civil rights cases. Scott soon told Lowe how much she wanted to attend the College of Arts and Sciences, which still rarely admitted women as four-year students. Lowe decided to represent Scott and three other women in their efforts to gain admission into the college on the same grounds as male applicants. "I tried to get an appointment to appear before a Board of Visitors meeting, but no one would give us an audience," Lowe told *UVA Lawyer* in 1996. "We felt we had no recourse but to file suit."

University officials were already discussing full coeducation. The Supreme Court ruling against "separate but equal" education could apply to gender as well as to race. Other all-male schools were moving swiftly toward coeducation—Princeton, Yale, Dartmouth. President Shannon appointed French professor T. Braxton Woody to head a committee to investigate the admission of women to the College of Arts and Sciences. An alumnus from the 1920s, Woody had opposed coeducation for years—which was in part why Shannon chose him. "With the committee I'm going to give him," Shannon told his executive assistant, Francis L. Berkeley Jr., "he will change his mind."

Woody invited alumni to comment on the need for coeducation at the university. He received 101 letters in response. Thirty alumni—21 male, 9 female—favored coeducation; 69 male and 2 female alumni did not. He also invited the faculty to comment, and of the 157 letters that came in response, 141 encouraged coeducation of the College of Arts and Sciences. Only 9 expressed a negative opinion; 6 seemed indifferent. The student honor committee prepared a report, leaning heavily on a 1964 study that found honor codes more effective at single-sex, particularly male, schools than at

The Shannon family, 1969. *The father of five daughters, President Edgar Shannon oversaw the evolution of the University of Virginia from a primarily male school to a coeducational university.*

coeducational colleges. A leader of the Raven Society expressed a qualified vote for coeducation, as long as change came gradually. The 1968 April Fool's Day issue of the *Cavalier Daily* spread banner headlines across the front page: "University to Become Fully Co-Educational for Next Session Despite Alumni Opposition." To illustrate the story the newspaper ran a photograph of Edgar Shannon, his wife, Eleanor, and their five young daughters. The spoof quoted Shannon as saying he was pleased that his daughters could now attend the university.

In November 1968, Woody and his committee recommended rescinding restrictions on the admission of women to the College of Arts and Sciences. The Board of Visitors agreed to measured and gradual coeducation. First the wives and daughters of students and faculty members could enter the college in the 1969–70 school year (a small gain, since faculty relatives were already admitted and few undergraduate men had wives or daughters). Then admission was to be granted to a few more women, slowly building over the years, to a projected total of 35 percent of the student body.

Lowe filed suit on behalf of Virginia Anne Scott and three other women in federal court in the spring of 1969. The judge granted a temporary injunction in their favor, and in September 1969 Scott entered the University of Virginia, a symbolic step toward full coeducation. The other three women chose not to attend the university.

A plan of female education has never been a subject of systematic contemplation with me.

— THOMAS JEFFERSON, 1818

That fall, eleven women—Scott, one faculty wife, and nine upper-class transfer students—entered the College of Arts and Sciences. In 1970, 350 women entered the college; in 1971, 450 entered. In 1972, the first year of open female admissions, 45 percent of the first-year class were women. Dormitories on Alderman Road were designated coeducational, their upper floors refurbished for women. Renovations lagged behind admissions. For a few years, houseplants grew in the urinals.

Faculty Gains

From the mid-1960s on, the Commonwealth's Eminent Scholars Fund allowed the university to offer competitive salaries and research support to

hire new scholars and build a nationally prominent faculty. The idea was first conceived during Colgate Darden's administration and was finally adopted by the state in 1964. According to the new program, when a private donor established an endowment for faculty salary, the state would match that income—providing a significant increase in gains to the university and an excellent selling point for fundraisers. "We worked up a plan," says Vincent Shea, bursar under Darden and Shannon, "and it was appropriated not just for the University of Virginia but for all the state institutions of higher learning."

At the same time, the university developed its Center for Advanced Studies. When the National Science Foundation offered thirty science development awards to support laboratory research, the university submitted an unusual application. Instead of funneling grant money into existing laboratories, it would create a Center for Advanced Studies in the Sciences. Top scholars would be appointed as center fellows for three years, receiving higher-than-average salaries and research support. In 1967 the center began appointing fellows in the humanities and social sciences as well, a strategy that worked even

better than that in the sciences, according to W. Dexter Whitehead, the center's founding director. Over the years since its founding, the Center for Advanced Studies has drawn dozens of notable professors to the university, including the geneticist Robert Kretsinger, the historian Norman Graebner, the political scientist Matthew Holden, the psychologist Mary Ainsworth, the materials scientist Edgar A. Starke Jr., and the poet Rita Dove. In 1994, recognizing how the center's influence paralleled Edgar Shannon's efforts to build the academic stature of the university, the Board of Visitors renamed it the Shannon Center for Advanced Studies.

Fredson Bowers, English professor.
Under Bowers's leadership as an enterprising departmental chair, the university's Department of English gained a national reputation by the 1970s. Bowers also exerted influence internationally in the field of editing literary texts.

The Bowers Era

During the 1960s one department in particular raised the sights of the entire university. Most attribute the swift advance of the English department to Fredson T. Bowers, a scholar renowned for his theory and practice of editing literary texts. His book *Principles of Bibliographic Description* became the central reference for scholars working on the textual editing of manuscripts and early literary editions. Managing a staff that included editors, librarians, young faculty, and graduate students, Bowers produced authoritative texts that cut across time, genre, and geography, including works by the Elizabethan playwrights Christopher Marlowe and Thomas Dekker; the American authors Nathaniel Hawthorne, Walt Whitman, and Stephen Crane; the philosopher William James; and the novelist Vladimir Nabokov. Through his own work ethic, productivity, and style, Bowers set standards that were hard to meet. "He was feared, sometimes hated, sometimes mocked in fear, always held in awe," recalled Roy Flannagan, a student of Bowers's in the 1960s.

As chairman of the English department from 1961 to 1968, Bowers hired a team of literary scholars that brought the department from relative obscurity into the nation's top ten. Most of the faculty recruited by Bowers continued to distinguish themselves: Irvin Ehrenpreis, as a biographer and critic of Jonathan Swift; Martin Battestin, as an editor and biographer of Henry Fielding; Robert W. Langbaum, as a critic of modern literature, both poetry and fiction; Arthur Kirsch, as a Shakespeare scholar; J. C. Levenson, as an authority on Henry Adams and Stephen Crane; Ralph Cohen, as a scholar of eighteenth-century literature who founded the groundbreaking journal *New Literary History;* and Raymond Nelson, as a scholar of modern American poetry, who also served as dean of the College of Arts and Sciences from 1989 to 1997.

Many fondly remember Bowers's schemes to hire them—like the letter sent in 1966 to E. D. Hirsch Jr., a literary theorist now known for his best-selling *Cultural Literacy.* Hirsch was then an assistant professor at Yale, drawing attention with his new book *Validity in Interpretation* and already considering offers from the Universities of California and Pennsylvania. Knowing that Hirsch had served in the navy, Bowers pasted four stamps on the envelope. Stamps picturing Virginia and the navy he attached right-side up; stamps picturing Pennsylvania and California, upside down. When Bowers welcomed Hirsch to the faculty the next fall, he asked for the envelope back, to add to his own stamp collection.

A New Building for New Sciences

In 1963 departments representing the "life sciences"—biology and psychology—moved into Gilmer Hall, an obliquely shaped modern building very different from other classroom buildings on the university grounds. "I hope the chaos on the outside isn't reflected on the inside," the *Cavalier Daily* quoted one architecture professor as saying. Dietrich Bodenstein, chair of biology, argued that it was the "best-designed functional building" for biology at any university of the day.

The functions for which Bodenstein wished the new building designed were cellular studies, a new domain in biology, superseding the traditions of natural history and classification memorialized in Brooks Hall. As Bodenstein explained this revolution in science, "Before, we asked: How does it look? Now, we ask: Why is it that way?" Typifying the new approach was the work of the cell geneticist Oscar Miller. Joining the faculty in 1973, Miller developed a revolutionary procedure, dubbed "Miller spreading," which unwound chromosomes and separated individual genes, allowing a scientist to witness DNA replication through an electron microscope. In

Gilmer Hall's other wing, psychology faculty specialized in infant and family studies, led by Mavis Hetherington and Mary Ainsworth, both of whom joined the faculty in the early 1970s. Hetherington, drawing results from large-scale observational studies, explored the dynamics of divorce and step-parenting in the lives of American children. Ainsworth focused on mother-infant bonding, analyzing what she called "the strange situation"

between mother and child, in that close affection in the early years facilitates independence and separation as the child matures. In 1983 Sandra Scarr, an expert in the effects of day care on children, joined the department, adding another strong female teacher-scholar to the psychology department's ranks.

Seven Society symbol graces University Hall. *University Hall, an athletic arena designed to seat nine thousand, opened in 1965 with a winning basketball game against the University of Kentucky. In a matter of months, the symbol for the Seven Society had appeared mysteriously atop the arena's seashell roof.*

A Changed University

Edgar Shannon announced his intention to retire from the presidency in 1974, to return to teaching and to his work on the letters of Alfred, Lord Tennyson. In a number of ways, the University of Virginia was not the same institution at which he had been inaugurated fifteen years before. Between 1960 and 1970 the student population had more than doubled. University Hall opened in 1965, a huge new arena for athletic and cultural events. A new wing of Alderman Library had opened in 1967, with shelf space for a million more volumes. By 1970 new degree programs had been established in interdisciplinary majors like Asian, Afro-American, Latin American, and Russian studies; in new technological fields like computer science, biomedical engineering, and urban design; and in more languages, including Chinese, Japanese, Sanskrit, Hindi, Polish, and Serbo-Croatian.

Change, a national educational journal, characterized the University of Virginia of 1972 as "a first-rate academic institution according to all the traditional barometers of academic excellence." The decade before had seen expansion, diversification, and specialization, and all the while the University of Virginia was gaining in academic stature.

BEYOND THE LAWN

Jefferson's architectural master-piece presented a challenge to succeeding generations as they worked to expand his university. "Architects designing new university buildings are caught in a dilemma," says Murray Howard, curator of the academical village. "Do you compete with, or for that matter marry with, the great central architecture of the university? Or do you create the best of your own time?" In a sense, one can study America's architectural history in the sequence of buildings added to the University of Virginia since Jefferson's time.

Stanford White's re-created Rotunda and, more visibly today, his president's house and the three buildings at the south end of the Lawn—Rouss Hall, Cabell Hall, and Cocke Hall—represent late nineteenth-century neoclassicism, echoing Jefferson's own interest in elements of Greek and Roman architecture. In the 1920s, the architecture professor Sidney Fiske Kimball continued use of the neoclassical style in his designs for the McIntire Amphitheater, just outside the Lawn, and Memorial Gymnasium. In the 1930s Edmund S. Campbell, like Kimball a faculty member keenly interested in Jefferson, restated the neoclassical aesthetic in, among other buildings, the Bayly Museum and the commerce school's Monroe Hall.

In the mid-twentieth century, American architects worked to break free of classicism. Modernist design influenced new buildings added to the university's grounds: Gilmer

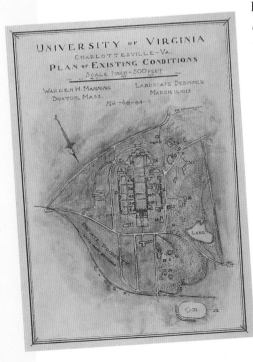

Top: Sidney Fiske Kimball. Left: Planning map, 1913. Above: New Cabell Hall under construction in foreground, new dormitories in background, 1952.

Above: Edmund S. Campbell. Left: Campbell Hall, School of Architecture, opened in 1970.

Visiting architect I. M. Pei, 1976

Hall, Jordan Hall, Culbreth Theater, buildings for education and English, and, in 1970, the complex of buildings designed for architecture, art, and the fine arts library. Using stark geometric lines and experimenting with interior space, the architecture building was considered by J. Norwood Bosserman, then the dean of the architecture school, to be "the most significant building constructed at the University since Jefferson designed and built the original academical village." Housed in that building, under the leadership of Deans Bosserman and Jaquelin T.

Robertson through the 1980s, the architecture school grew in size, diversity of interests, and reputation.

A growing university raised questions of location as well as of style. When the law school and the graduate business school outgrew Clark Hall and Monroe Hall, respectively, the decision was made to establish a new center of activity not contiguous with the original Lawn. The university had already grown in that direction, developing the Copeley Hill housing area after World War II and constructing University Hall in the early 1960s. By the mid-1970s the new North Grounds consisted of the law school, the graduate business school, and the judge advocate general's school (the army's center for law education, affiliated with the university since World War II).

The 1976 renovation of the Rotunda marked a new era of respect for classically inspired architecture. The Balfour Addition to Monroe Hall, which provided expanded facilities for the McIntire School

of Commerce, opened in 1987. Bryan Hall, designed for the English department, opened in 1995. Declared the final building ever to be added within sight of Jefferson's own Lawn, Bryan Hall was designed by the internationally renowned architect Michael Graves, a leader in the postmodern return to classical lines and architectural elements.

As the law school and the Darden School grew, a plan developed for significant expansion of the North Grounds in the late 1990s. New buildings reflected the same postmodern respect for neoclassical design. Expanding into the building formerly dedicated to the Darden School, the law school renovated both buildings, adjoined them with halls to the north and south, and added a reading room and pavilion. Simultaneously, the Darden School built a complex of new buildings, including classrooms and offices, plus living and dining facilities for its visiting executive programs.

Below: Fiske Kimball's McIntire Amphitheater and Bryan Hall. Right: Darden School foyer.

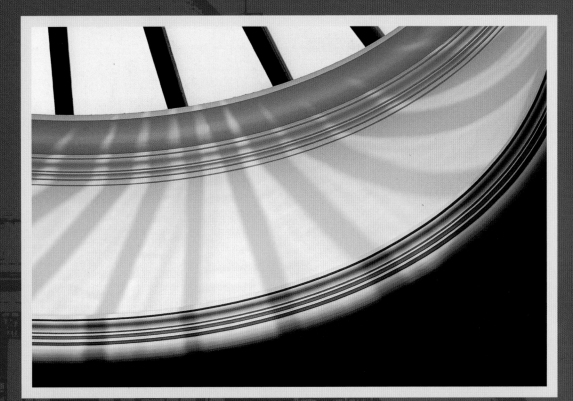

Restoring Ideals

Frank L. Hereford Jr., fifth president of the university

Until 1950 the office of the president occupied the upstairs floor of Pavilion IV, into which Alderman had moved when he first took on the job. When Professor William Thornton died, thus vacating Pavilion VIII, Colgate Darden moved the president's office there, occupying the full building. As the president's staff grew, even larger quarters were needed. When Darden asked how university buildings could accommodate his growing staff, architecture professor Frederick D. Nichols suggested creating presidential office space in the Rotunda according to its original Jeffersonian design. "Once again," Nichols wrote in 1961, the Rotunda "would become the focal point of the University."

Few in the 1960s were aware that the Rotunda they knew was not the one Jefferson had designed. Architects Nichols and William B. O'Neal published information about the differences. Students initiated the Restoration Ball, a formal dance first held in 1964 to raise money and awareness. State appropriations to shore up the dome joined a two-million-dollar federal grant for historic preservation. In 1973 the Rotunda closed its doors to the public for restoration, to reopen in 1976, the nation's bicentennial year.

Decisions had to be made throughout the renovation process. Many structural details

1980

- *16,400 students*

- *1,500 faculty members*

- *5,000 staff members*

- *Lawn rooms: $776 per nine-month year*

- *Average annual expenses for an undergraduate: $3,200*

Restoration Ball. *Students supported plans to restore the Rotunda to its original Jeffersonian design by organizing an annual formal dance, the Restoration Ball, starting in 1964.*

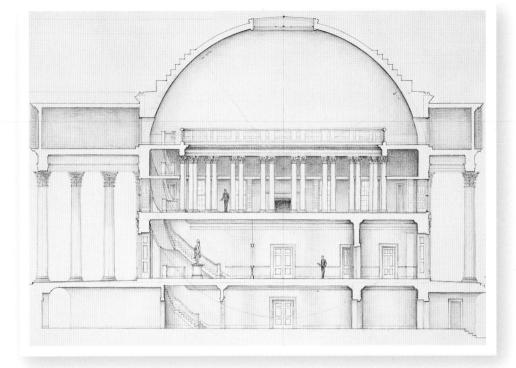

Restoring Jefferson's Rotunda.
After the 1895 fire, Stanford White redesigned the Rotunda's interior. Eighty years later, the university was rebuilding the Rotunda once again, this time with the intention of restoring the building to its original Jeffersonian design (right), as conceived by architect and alumnus Louis Ballou.

had never been written down, by either Stanford White or Jefferson. For example, the design of the oculus at the center of the dome had to be reconstructed using the original shipping receipts. "We had no information on the shape of the [original] skylight—how many divisions it had or anything about the slope," project architect Louis Ballou explained. Jefferson's drawing showed a skylight sixteen feet across. The original one leaked and was soon replaced, but the intention in the 1970s was to reconstruct a leakproof version of Jefferson's original. Early records showed the purchase of three trapezoidal pieces of glass, about two feet long. "We assumed that was the largest piece used," said Ballou. "From that assumption we could calculate the number of panels and the height of the skylight."

At one point the Rotunda was nothing but a hollow silo of brick, eighty feet tall and seventy feet across. As workers stripped away structures added in the 1890s' reconstruction, they revealed features from Jefferson's day, among them stone-lined ovens in the walls, presumably used by early chemistry classes.

Jefferson's notes on the oculus. *Historical research informed many details of the Rotunda restoration, such as the reconstruction of the dome's oculus. The shape and size of its glass panes were determined by studying Jefferson's notes and drawings together with sales receipts from the time.*

Tear down the new, rebuild the old. *To restore the Rotunda, contractors were forced first to strip the building down to a shell. Workers removed the Galt statue of Jefferson from the Rotunda for only the second time. Eighty years before, it had been heaved down the stairs during the great fire.*

The dome's exterior. *In shape, and even in color, the dome of the Rotunda changed during the 1976 restoration. Stanford White's design (inset) made the dome more conical, but the restored shape more closely resembled the top of a sphere. White had roofed the Rotunda with copper, which aged with a green patina. After research and testing a variety of colors (above), university officials decided to paint the restored dome roof white.*

Other details could not be traced back to Jeffersonian origins. Stanford White had roofed the Rotunda in copper, which with age had developed a green patina. Jefferson-era evidence suggested a white dome, since only white paint shows up in early lists of materials. Most likely, the dome was painted numerous colors over its 150 years. In September 1975 a variety of roof coatings were tested. For a few weeks the dome had stripes. The final choice of white arose as much from modern taste as it did from historical accuracy.

The restored Rotunda opened on Thomas Jefferson's birthday, 13 April 1976. The American Institute of Architects cited the academical village—the Rotunda, the Lawn and Ranges, and the pavilions and hotels—as the nation's most significant architectural achievement. The *New York Times* architecture critic Ada Louise Huxtable called a visit to the Rotunda "a trip to the source to touch base with the beginnings of the new nation." Queen Elizabeth II included the university as one of only five stops during her state visit.

Growth Factors

By the 1970s the university had grown in size, stature, and character. Under legislative pressure to admit more Virginians, out-of-state student numbers changed from 47 percent in 1959 to 30 percent in 1973. Enrollment tripled in fifteen years, from fewer than 5,000 in 1960 to 10,000 in 1970 and 15,000 in 1975, with an ultimate size of 18,000 set for sometime in the 1980s. Growth again raised controversy, as it had in the 1950s. Polled in 1971, students voted 72 percent against expanding further.

Faculty numbers increased as well. In 1973 more than half the full-time faculty members were younger than forty. Faculty salaries nearly doubled between 1960 and 1970, becoming nationally competitive. Research funding grew. Departments began to appear in the national rankings, English leading the way. The University of Virginia was on its way to becoming—to use the term coined in 1972 by Clark Kerr, president of the University of California—a "multiversity."

Queen Elizabeth visits. *As part of the nation's bicentennial celebration, in July 1976 Elizabeth II visited the University of Virginia. She and Prince Philip attended a luncheon in the Dome Room then greeted a crowd of 18,000 gathered on the Lawn to see her.*

Against growth. *From the Darden presidency on, while administrators and legislators have favored increasing the number of students admitted to the university, the students themselves have often disagreed, as seen from this protest of the early 1980s.*

President Hereford

When the Board of Visitors selected Frank L. Hereford Jr. as the fifth president of the university, student leaders were surprised, but those in inner administrative circles were not. Hereford had been a close contender for the presidency when Shannon was selected. A Virginian with three physics degrees from the university and a protégé of Jesse Beams's, Hereford had held numerous administrative positions, including that of provost under Edgar Shannon. He was an eager fan of athletics and a member of Farmington Country Club. Alumni of the 1940s and 1950s considered him one of them.

The Herefords at Carr's Hill.
Ann and Frank Hereford worked together to bring alumni and friends into contact with the university.

"Frank Hereford worked at molding alumni relationships," recalls William H. Fishback, head of information services for the university at the time. "He took a whole year before he took office as president to travel and build up alumni relations. We called it his 'red shirt' year. His presidency was an era of good feeling among the alumni."

A Society of Alumni dated back to 1838, when twenty-seven graduates gathered in the Rotunda to celebrate on the Fourth of July. By 1974, when Hereford came into office, the alumni body numbered about fifteen thousand. At the end of his presidency, ten years later, alumni numbers had grown to more than ninety thousand. Several schools—notably law, medicine, and the Darden School—supported alumni offices of their own, but Hereford urged them to band together, recognizing their common loyalty to the university.

Alumni communications.
In 1894 the university began distributing the Alumni Bulletin, *shown here, written and edited by faculty members including Dean James M. Page, who was for years the volunteer alumni secretary. When Lewis D. Crenshaw came to relieve Dean Page of alumni duties, he initiated the* Alumni News, *which first appeared in 1913. For nine years the two publications existed side by side, until in 1924 the faculty diverted funds from the* Bulletin *to found the* Virginia Quarterly Review.

To Hereford goes much of the credit for the success of the university's capital campaign of the 1980s, the largest ever launched by a public university at the time. "When I took office, two-thirds of our endowment came from large gifts given by outsiders to the university," says Hereford. "My thought was that we have got to gain more support from our alumni." By 1984 the campaign had raised almost $150 million, far beyond the initial $90 million goal.

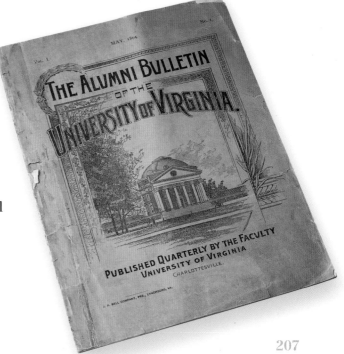

Alumni leadership. *Malcolm "Mac" Luck (center), director of the Alumni Association from 1930 to 1958, oversaw the 1936 purchase and the 1950 expansion of Alumni Hall, originally the home of the Zeta Beta Tau fraternity. Below, one of a series of six Wedgwood plates produced in 1939.*

As the campaign reached its climax, manifested in the financing of a new seven-story, $200-million hospital, Hereford announced his intention to leave the presidency and return to teaching physics. His efforts most visibly had been to reach out and engage alumni, but during the years of his administration, the academic strengths of the university had continued building. A new undergraduate library, named after long-time librarian Harry Clemons, opened in 1980. In 1982 the *New York Times Selective Guide to Colleges* gave Virginia a five-star rating for academics and quality of life. "He completed something he had started as provost under Shannon," says Alexander G. Gilliam, who served as assistant to President Hereford. "He built up the faculty."

Athletic Prowess

In 1974 a new basketball coach arrived at the university—Terry Holland, from Davidson College. He hired a black assistant coach, the university's first, Bill Cofield. In May 1979 Holland recruited seven-foot-four Ralph Sampson, one of the nation's most promising high school players. During the next four years Sampson's team made it to the NCAA Final Four, never winning the tournament but rousing more Cavalier spirit than the university had seen in decades. Debbie Ryan started coaching women's basketball in 1977; in 1978 the university hosted the ACC women's tournament, and in 1979 the team started on a winning streak that continued into the 1990s. Bruce Arena started coaching men's soccer in 1978; in his first season the team won nine out of thirteen games and tied two more, the start of a winning streak that lasted into the 1990s as well.

Meanwhile, in football, Virginia's team had played only one winning season since 1952. In 1982 George Welsh—a quiet, stern perfectionist, according to the *Cavalier Daily*—started coaching football. That first season he agreed to let Ted Turner's new cable television network broadcast a night game—the first ever in Scott Stadium—against Clemson University. The university rented massive spotlights to illuminate the field. Clemson won, 48-0. "Too bad the lights worked," wrote the *Cavalier Daily* the next day. "We are a terrible football team," the paper quoted Welsh as saying. In two years' time, though, the team had started winning. Invited to the Peach Bowl in Atlanta on New Year's Eve, 1984—once again before national television cameras—Virginia's football team beat Purdue, 27-24.

Tallest Lawn resident, 1983. *Named national basketball player of the year for three years straight, Ralph Sampson consistently broke scoring records and instilled a new sense of excitement among Cavalier fans. He lived on the Lawn during his fourth year at the university. He was recruited by the Houston Rockets and named rookie of the year in 1984. After a knee injury forced Sampson to retire from basketball, he opened a sportswear company in Richmond.*

The Demise of Easters

As athletics revived at Virginia, another tradition ground to a halt. In 1982 university officials banned Easters. The vernal celebration was a long-held tradition, with springtime dances dating back to the nineteenth century. In 1919, recalled T. Braxton Woody, "Easters was not a weekend, it was Easter Week. A solid week of formal dances, because all the dances were formal…. You never cut class. You'd go to class, in your tux, of course. You'd answer the roll and then you'd immediately go to sleep, but you were there." By the mid-1970s Easters annually drew thousands of party-seekers into the area of Rugby Road and Madison Bowl—and not just University of Virginia students. In 1975, after a weekend of rock-and-roll and mud-caked streakers, President Hereford announced that the university was reconsidering its approach to Easters. The "best party in the country" was turning into a liability.

A student committee formed, promising to take control and design an event with decorum. They proposed that the university revert to "Easters Week," to offer a wider variety of events. The effect was simply to lengthen the party. In 1979, prohibited from partying near the university, a thousand people flocked to a farm five miles south of Charlottesville. The next year word had spread and cars jammed Old Lynchburg Road for three hours straight. When Albemarle County insisted that the farm owner buy a permit to host so many guests, off-grounds Easters met its end. Student frolics continued at Foxfield, though, where tailgate party-goers watched steeplechase races each fall and spring.

Mudslide in Mad Bowl. *Springtime festivities, nick-named Easters, had been a long-held tradition. By the mid-1970s, the tradition included all-night parties, loud rock and roll, and mudslides in Madison Bowl. In 1979 university officials put an end to the celebrations.*

Issues of Inclusion

As dean of admissions from 1975 to 1982, John T. Casteen, later university president, spent many evenings traveling throughout Virginia with Lloyd Ricks, a black educator and an assistant dean of admissions. Ricks and Casteen met African American families at schools, churches, and community centers. "The YWCA in Roanoke on a Sunday night, for example," says Casteen. "On a typical night you might see just five or six families." Their mission was to communicate to African American families that their sons and daughters were welcome at the University of Virginia.

For African American students to feel comfortable and do their best at the university, their numbers needed to grow. Fewer than five hundred black students attended the university in 1975, scarcely more than 3 percent of the total student population. That year the Black Student Alliance formed and formally proposed that the university establish an office of minority affairs. One year later the Office of Afro-American Affairs opened on Dawson's Row. William M. Harris, a professor of architecture (and twin brother of Wesley Harris, the first African American resident of the Lawn), was named the university's first dean of Afro-American affairs.

Many saw the need to build a larger faculty contingent of African

Celebrating diversity. *Efforts of admissions officers, including John Casteen (above, inset) brought more African American students to the university. As the university culture developed to include minorities—through the establishment of an Office of Afro-American Affairs, headed by a dean, and through the founding of the Carter G. Woodson Institute for Afro-American and African Studies—the colors and rhythms of world cultures came to life at the university.*

**Expanding the scholarly
community.** *Armstead L.
Robinson, director of the university's Carter G. Woodson
Institute from 1981 until 1995,
emphasized the importance
of educating young African
American scholars.*

American scholars as well. In 1980 the black historian Armstead Robinson was hired to head a new institute for Afro-American and African studies. Paul Gaston, a Southern historian and integration activist since the 1950s, had been urging the establishment of black studies at the university for years, inspired by Robinson's book *Black Studies in the University,* which argued the importance of building an interdisciplinary community of schol-ars in the field. The institute that Robinson headed, in 1982 named the Carter G. Woodson Institute after the pioneering black historian, inspired a constellation of courses across the university curriculum and supported young scholars researching topics as diverse as, for example, the metaphor of paradise in Caribbean literature and educational reform in Virginia.

The university attracted female students with ease, but the number of women faculty did not increase proportionately. In 1970 fewer than 5 per-cent of the College of Arts and Sciences faculty were women. Out of a total of 483, only 23 were women, only 10 of those women had appointments at the level of assistant professor or above, and only 6 had tenure. By 1983 the proportion of women faculty in arts and sciences had grown to 18 per-cent, but still only 15 of the total 106 had tenure. By 1990, of the College of Arts and Sciences's 631 faculty members, 122—nearly 20 percent—were women, 36 with tenured appointments as associate or full professors. Yet of the more than 200 endowed professorships granted to esteemed faculty at the university in 1990, only 10 were held by female faculty. Only a few women were moving from the faculty into the administration—Mavis Hetherington had been chair of psychology, Barbara Nolan was acting chair of English, and Marita McClymonds was chair of music.

Other minorities were finding a voice by the mid-1980s. In 1973 the student council refused to grant activities funds to the Gay Student Union, designating it a "social" organization for a select membership, not a "service" organization for all students. Ten years later the student council reversed its stand: not only did it recognize the Lesbian and Gay Student Union as a service organization, but in 1986 it considered withholding funds from the Campus Crusade for Christ for publicly disavowing homo-sexuality. In the late 1980s faculty and staff campaigned for the university to expand its nondiscrimination policy to include gender and sexual orientation. Their success, achieved in 1991, prompted the official founding of a faculty, staff, and graduate-student association dedicated to issues affecting sexual minorities.

President O'Neil

The search for a new president in 1984 resulted in the selection of Robert M. O'Neil, president of the University of Wisconsin, as sixth president of the University of Virginia. Educated at Harvard, O'Neil was a specialist in First Amendment rights who had taught law at the University of California at Berkeley and Indiana University. Not since Edwin Alderman had the university appointed a president without any prior connections to the Commonwealth or to the University of Virginia. "The search committee thought that it had shown great maturity in going outside the university to select a president," says Alexander G. Gilliam, who served as secretary to that committee. O'Neil, says Gilliam, "knew more of the academic world than any of his predecessors, and he knew less about this place than any of his predecessors."

Robert M. O'Neil, sixth president of the university

O'Neil singled out minority affairs, women's issues, and substance abuse as three areas of continuing concern at the university. He created task-force committees, charging them to study the ramifications of each of these three problems. Each task force gathered information; interviewed students, staff, and faculty; and submitted reports, all calling for institutional change. Some effects were immediate. In 1987 the university established the Holland Scholarships, to attract black students with strong academic records and leadership qualities. To support faculty and staff women and their families, the university opened an employee day-care center. A fully funded Women's Center opened in 1989, with a full-time director, Sharon Davie. And a new institute tackled substance abuse—locally through counseling and education programs, and nationally through sponsored research. O'Neil's task forces continued their work through the late 1980s.

A Tibetan presence on the Lawn. *In the 1970s and 1980s, the religious studies department developed an especially strong program in Tibetan studies. Visiting Tibetan Buddhist monks coached American students in the finer points of debate within their ancient tradition (above). In November 1998 the Dalai Lama, shown here with Bishop Desmond Tutu, was among the Nobel Peace Prize laureates who gathered for a conference at the university.*

Studies in Conscience

Three new fields of study—biomedical ethics, Tibetan studies, and environmental sciences—and a new degree program—the master of arts in teaching—developed at the university during Robert O'Neil's presidency, paralleling the social conscience of his administration in the realms of scholarship and teaching.

Medical ethics had long been a field of interest at the University of Virginia, dating back to 1970, when Joseph Fletcher, author of the influential *Situation Ethics,* had taught medical, law, and liberal arts students, raising issues then rarely discussed like abortion, euthanasia, and cloning. In 1989 John Fletcher (not related to Joseph), also teaching students in both the medical school and the arts and sciences, founded the Center for Biomedical Ethics. Fletcher worked with James Childress, a professor of religious studies, to introduce ethics into the university's medical curriculum. The center also offered short courses on biomedical ethics for visiting physicians and coached doctors at the university hospital on how to resolve ethical dilemmas raised by advanced medical technologies.

It became almost commonplace by the early 1990s to see Tibetan Buddhist monks, heads shorn, draped in saffron robes, walking across the Lawn, drawn to the University of Virginia by the library's rich holdings and the presence of P. Jeffrey Hopkins, friend, translator, and interpreter of the Dalai Lama.

Tibetan materials were rare worldwide and virtually nonexistent in Chinese-occupied Tibet. When Richard B. Martin, a specialist in South Asian bibliography, joined the library staff in 1967, his colleague John Wyllie had already enrolled the university in a federal program that, in essence, traded American food staples for Third World printed material. This way, from the early 1960s on, the University of Virginia collected Tibetan sacred books and commentaries, including many *bejas*—wide, squat stacks of paper, printed with wood blocks and wrapped in colorful cloth and ribbons. Martin actively acquired Tibetan works beyond those that came through the federal exchange, and by 1990 the University of Virginia owned about 80 percent of the entire corpus of traditional Tibetan Buddhist literature. Jeffrey Hopkins joined the faculty in 1973, and the university's religious studies department developed courses in Tibetan language, literature, religion, and culture. Since then the Dalai Lama has visited the university several times, including an appearance during a 1998 gathering of Nobel Peace Prize laureates.

Man of Many Devices

Director of admissions in the Darden administration, Raymond C. Bice helped market the university to a broader student population in the 1950s. Bice also taught Psychology 101, in which he demonstrated his famous "Bice devices," homemade machines designed to convey principles of perception and cognition. He offered the popular course from 1948 to 1994 and estimates that he taught a total of 27,000 students. In 1991 he was appointed university history officer, a post he held until his retirement in 1998.

Interdisciplinary study of the environment may be a commonplace today, but it was a new idea when, in 1969, the geologist Robert Dolan encouraged the university to found a Department of Environmental Studies. "We were one of the first universities to use the term 'environmental sciences' in connection with an academic program, and we were, as I recall, the first in the nation to offer degrees, including the Ph.D.," says Dolan. Combining geology and geography, the university created a new department to encompass ecology, hydrology, and climatology, as well as any new earth sciences that might evolve in years to come.

Research in environmental studies at the university was conducted on both local and global levels in the 1980s. Students and faculty, including Dolan, used global-positioning satellite systems to track coastal erosion along Virginia's eastern shore. James M. Galloway initiated long-term studies of acid rain in the Shenandoah National Park. Computer algorithms in Hank Shugart's laboratory generated patterns of environmental progression centuries into the future. Shugart's simulations were applied to gypsy moth damage in Virginia forests, to rain-forest growth in Australia, and to pollution problems in the forests of Switzerland. African nations used his models to develop resource-management plans stretching into the twenty-first century.

In the 1980s, public concern over education was growing. The president's commission on education had warned in 1983 that the United States was "a nation at risk," on a "rising tide of mediocrity." Since its founding in the first decade of the twentieth century, the Curry School of Education had specialized in educating administrators—counselors, principals and headmasters, superintendents, and educational specialists in fields like special learning, speech pathology, and audiology. In answer to public concern, the Curry School renovated its teacher-training curriculum, from 1985 on requiring every student to complete a five-year program that combined learning theory, teaching practice, and courses equivalent to those required for a four-year liberal arts degree. Graduates earned a bachelor of arts in a subject area and a master of arts in teaching, and the intent was that they entered the classroom solidly grounded in the subjects they were to teach.

Further Restorations

Although the plan had been to move the president's office into the Rotunda, when the time came, the great oval rooms seemed neither large enough nor suitably designed for modern administrative offices. Instead, the president's office moved off the Lawn, across University Avenue to Madison Hall. Alumni remembered seeing Alderman, Newcomb, Darden, Shannon, and Hereford at work in their pavilion offices or walking the colonnades of the Lawn. Now the president worked apart from the day-to-day on-grounds traffic. "The move from Pavilion VIII to Madison Hall created a geographic and symbolic distance," says O'Neil. "Madison Hall is isolated."

In another way, though, moving the president's office off the Lawn served to build community. Once Pavilion VIII was vacated, work began to renovate its interior for classrooms and student meeting rooms downstairs and a faculty apartment upstairs—following the original intention for it and the other pavilions. With the Pavilion VIII restoration, the university embarked on a forty-year plan, a comprehensive effort to modernize the buildings for safety and comfort and at the same time to restore and conserve their historic and architectural identities. In 1987 UNESCO added the Lawn to its World Heritage List. In 1995 the university received an honor award from the American Institute of Architects, recognizing its stewardship of "the most important architectural ensemble in America."

Jefferson 1743-1826 Virginia Rotunda

Architecture USA 15c

Commemorative appearance. *The Rotunda and academical village garnered national and international accolades for architecture from 1976 on. In 1979 the Rotunda was one of four buildings chosen for a set of U.S. postage stamps commemorating American architecture.*

Pavilion restoration. *Once the Rotunda was restored, university architects turned their attention to the rest of the academical village, instating a comprehensive plan for restoration and conservation. Here, for example, repairs are being made to the decorative frieze of Pavilion II.*

The Rotunda and Lawn, monuments to the educational vision of Thomas Jefferson, welcomed as many as 130,000 visitors every year in the late 1990s. Student guides conducted tours daily, and in one first-floor oval room, the university installed a historical display about the university. Administrative offices lined the wings, but the oval rooms of the second floor, reserved for formal meetings, often went uninhabited. The Board of Visitors still convened in the East Oval Room, but from 1978 on, when new state laws opened their meetings to the press and the public, the meetings threatened to outgrow it.

The Rotunda stood at the head of the university Lawn but apart from the path of everyday life in the late twentieth century. Upstairs in the Dome Room, intended by Jefferson as the university library, an occasional student sat, quietly studying. Bookshelves around the room held editions belonging to the collection of the Rare Book School and Book Arts Press, brought to the university by Terry Belanger in 1992. A student might attend a lecture, a special dinner, or a formal dance in the Dome Room. Others came into the Rotunda out of curiosity and admiration. Sadly, however, some students graduated without ever having set foot in Jefferson's Rotunda.

The Electronic Academical Village

The first step toward computerization came in 1940, when the university acquired a machine to sort punched cards to track library circulation. Accounting records were mechanized in 1948, using equipment from International Business Machines. In 1954, the admissions director Raymond C. Bice began using the "Robotyper" to generate acceptance letters that looked individually typed but were in fact generated by the hundreds. Ten years later, university payroll accountants operated a $400,000 IBM data-processing system, which could punch 250 cards or perform 193,000 additions of eight-digit numbers in one minute. That same year, research faculty depended on the university's million-dollar Burroughs B5000 for computations. It was in that year as well that the

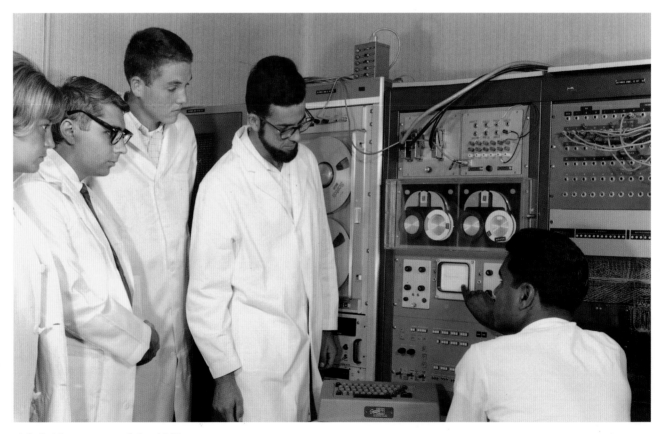

A hybrid computer of the 1960s

Computer technologies permeated every aspect of university life. In 1988 the university libraries initiated VIRGO, their on-line catalogue, and in 1998 the last oak cabinets with drawers full of index cards disappeared, making way for a café in the lobby of Alderman Library. Admissions applications and registration procedures went on-line in 1994; the offices of purchasing, human resources, and financial administration shifted from paperwork to Web-based electronic records in 1998. In 1995 the University Press of Virginia published a new edition of *Afro-American Sources in Virginia: A Guide to Manuscripts,* the first book published on-line by any university press. In 1998, *Yahoo! Internet Life* magazine ranked the University of Virginia the sixteenth "most wired" college in the country.

Each year from 1995 on new electronic teaching projects were supported by a university-wide teaching and technology initiative. Benjamin Ray, a professor of religious studies, created electronic exhibits with images, video clips,

university registrar, after lengthy consideration, began using students' social security numbers for registration and student records.

In the 1980s and 1990s, the rate of technological change at the University of Virginia multiplied. Focused commitment to technology development came through the 1992 appointment of Polley A. McClure as chief information officer and the creation of a division of information technology and communication. By 1997 more than eighty different institutional computing systems—storing records from career placement to parking, from room scheduling to personnel recruitment—had been connected to a fiber-optic backbone. Students worked in more than thirty computer laboratories across the grounds. Almost one hundred classrooms, two-thirds of all student rooms, and all research laboratories were linked to the network.

Benjamin Ray, professor of religious studies. Above right: Jerome McGann, professor of English, and a student.

and music to enhance his classroom discussions of African art and culture. Robert Ribando, a professor of engineering, developed software for his heat transfer class, so students could view computer models linking mathematical equations with the processes of conduction, convection, radiation, and condensation they express. Kathy Poole, a professor of landscape architecture, worked with students to link computer-based landscape, ecology, and civil engineering information into a three-dimensional animation of a stressed geographic area. Elliott Weiss showed computer simulations of manufacturing processes to his graduate business students, giving them virtual plant tours without leaving the Darden School.

The history professor Edward Ayers brought the new technologies of the Internet and CD-ROMs into play to refresh current notions of Southern history. Ayers and his graduate students built an interactive database of text and images to chronicle the daily life of two communities, South and North, during the Civil War. Thousands of sources, both public and private, including newspapers, letters, diaries, photographs, maps, church archives, and census and military records, were coded for access through the Valley of the Shadow Web site, making primary materials available to anyone studying the Civil War.

Ayers's Civil War project represents a new age of research and publishing, using the computer not simply to calculate but also to image, search, and connect. In the Electronic Text Center, opened in Alderman Library in 1992, the University of Virginia began building an electronic archive of literary and artistic masterpieces. Visitors to the Electronic Text Center—whether coming in person or connecting by computer—gain access to thousands of works of literature, art, and music. Scholars can conduct studies of rare manuscripts without touching the originals; they can build concordances of select words from vast bodies of literature electronically.

In 1993 the university established the Institute for Advanced Technology in the Humanities, which serves as research center for emerging technolo-

Silicon chip research, 1995

Donald Richards, professor of statistics

gies, including virtual reality and three-dimensional modeling, as they apply to the study of language, literature, and the arts. The institute has sponsored, among many other projects, Edward Ayers's Valley of the Shadow; the multimedia work of Jerome McGann, a professor of English, who uses hyperlinks to study connections between the art and literature of the Pre-Raphaelite artist Dante Gabriel Rossetti; and art historian John Dobbins's three-dimensional computer-generated models of the forum in ancient Pompeii. The institute hosts on-line discussions of art, literature, and culture and publishes *Postmodern Culture,* founded in 1990, the oldest electronic scholarly journal in the humanities.

A University of the Twenty-first Century

John T. Casteen III, sixth president of the university

In 1985 the University of Virginia figured prominently in a book entitled *The Nation's Top Public Ivys.* The phrase seemed appropriate. Ever since the correspondence between Thomas Jefferson and George Ticknor, the university had compared itself with Harvard, Yale, and Princeton Universities. Its academic accomplishments were now becoming competitive, and state support meant lower tuition. *Money* magazine consistently placed Virginia on its list of best college bargains from the mid-1980s on, and at the same time Virginia was moving up in the ranks of state universities in lists published annually by *U.S. News and World Report.* Individual departments and schools were rising in reputation as well. President George Bush seemed to confirm these judgments when he chose the University of Virginia as the location for a first-ever governors' summit on education in America, in September 1989.

As it entered the 1990s, the University of Virginia was drawing attention and acclaim. More than 17,000 high school seniors applied for admission in 1990; the university would accept only 2,560 of them. The law school alone sifted through 6,000 applications for 380 places that year. Admissions officers had to devise ways of choosing among thousands of honor roll applicants. The student body maintained academic strength and grew more diverse

1995

- **18,000 students**
- **2,400 faculty members**
- **3,900 staff members**
- **Lawn rooms: $2,158 per nine-month year**
- **University meal plan: $2,000 per nine-month year**

National education summit, 1989. *President George Bush chose the University of Virginia as the site to which he invited state governors to convene in a discussion of national education issues.*

Nobel Peace Prize laureates assemble. *For two days in November 1998, the university hosted a historic conference on human rights, conflict, and reconciliation. Nine world peacemakers attended, including seven recipients of the Nobel Peace Prize. Attending the conference were (front, left to right) Bobby Muller of the U.S. Vietnam Veterans Foundation and the International Campaign to Ban Landmines; Rigoberta Menchú Tum of Guatemala; Archbishop Desmond Tutu of South Africa; Betty Williams, formerly of Belfast, Northern Ireland; (back, left to right) Harn Yawnghwe, attending for Aung San Suu Kyi of Burma; José Ramos-Horta of East Timor; Jody Williams of the International Campaign to Ban Landmines; His Holiness, the Dalai Lama, spiritual leader of Tibet; and Oscar Arias Sánchez, former president of Costa Rica.*

at the same time, achieving the highest graduation rate for African American students of any college in the country by the late 1990s.

President Casteen

In 1989 Robert O'Neil resigned the presidency of the university to become director of the new Thomas Jefferson Center for the Protection of Free Expression, from which he could continue his work as scholar and ombudsman in the area of First Amendment rights. The job of leading the institution through the next decade went to John T. Casteen III, inaugurated as president in 1990.

Raised in Portsmouth, Virginia, Casteen attended the University of Virginia from 1961 to 1970, writing a Ph.D. dissertation on Old English poetry and working in the library on, among other things, the papers of Thomas Jefferson. He taught at the University of California at Berkeley, then returned to Virginia as dean of admissions until he was appointed Virginia's secretary of education. Then, after five years as president of the University of Connecticut, he accepted Virginia's offer to return as president.

A Virginian, an alumnus with political experience and an educational career that had taken him to the West and the Northeast, Casteen was a teacher, a scholar, and an administrator. His credentials satisfied many constituencies. During his inaugural address he looked out into the audience and singled out friends—T. Braxton Woody, Douglas Day, Fredson Bowers, Dumas Malone, B. F. D. Runk, Irby Cauthen—some known nationally, but all well known within University of Virginia circles. "There was a time when the University took pride in being the premier university in the South," he said in his inaugural address. "Those times have changed." Now, he implied, the University of Virginia was moving into a larger circle, establishing a reputation not only among southern universities but nationally and internationally as well.

Casteen's most immediate challenge came as the Commonwealth of Virginia reduced its appropriations for higher education. All told, state budget cuts between 1990 and 1992 represented a reduction of more than 20 percent, or fifty million dollars, in state support for the university. Similar funding cuts were taking place across the nation. Twenty-six state universities faced budget reductions in 1992. "The Public Ivy Is Withering," read a headline in *Newsweek* in April 1991.

The response at the University of Virginia was twofold. The university underwent a massive restructuring with an intent to streamline and reduce administration while protecting teaching and health care services as much as possible from the effects of budget cuts. Soon thereafter the university announced a new capital campaign. Initiated in 1994, the campaign's goal was revised upward to one billion dollars in 1998, making it one of the largest ever waged by a university, public or private. Both initiatives combined to form what President Casteen called "an effort to reform the University's basic finances," relying more than ever on endowment income, private giving, government grants, and private research contracts.

A Learning and Teaching Community

Like many other major universities in the late twentieth century, Virginia sought a balance between research and teaching. Alumni reminisced about intimate classes taught by the university's senior statesmen and feared their children and grandchildren might have to choose between crowded lectures or classes taught by graduate students. The ideal of an academical village, where students and faculty lived and learned together, inspired efforts in the 1990s to strengthen an undergraduate learning community.

Entering honors students had since 1960 been invited to become Echols scholars, living in a dormitory together, but it was not until 1986

Friends of the university. *Television anchorwoman Katie Couric (top, surrounded by students), a 1979 graduate of the College of Arts and Sciences, maintained strong ties with the university, delivering the valedictory address in 1992 and named the Women's Center's distinguished alumna in 1993. When a horseback-riding accident caused near-total paralysis, actor Christopher Reeve (above, with U.Va. nurse Joy Stockton) received medical treatment from neurosurgeon John Jane and his team at the university. After his recovery, Reeve devoted himself to heightening public awareness of spinal cord injury research. He delivered the university's valedictory address in 1995.*

New communities. *Building on the success of its first residential college, the university established Hereford College (above) in 1992. Seven years earlier the university opened the Maison Française (below) in Dr. Paul Barringer's house. Undergraduate and graduate students, faculty, and staff shared not only living space but intellectual and social activities, becoming an academic community within the larger university.*

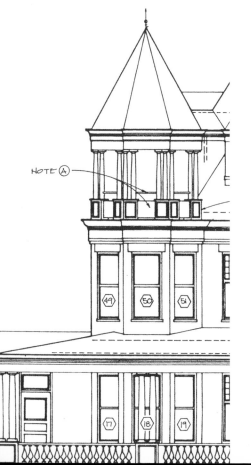

that other undergraduates could choose to live in a residential college. Situated in the oldest dormitories outside the original Lawn, Monroe Hill College (later renamed Brown College) brought students and faculty closer together, both in and outside the classroom. Faculty fellows lived at the college; members of the larger Charlottesville-Albemarle community also became college fellows, visiting regularly. The line between social and academic life blurred as faculty, students, staff, and visitors discussed intellectual topics at meals together. Brown College's success prompted the 1992 opening of another residential college, named after the past president Frank L. Hereford Jr., in newly built facilities.

Enthusiasm for learning communities strengthened language houses in the 1990s as well. The concept of student-faculty residences within which daily life is conducted in a foreign language was not new. Jefferson had hoped that one pavilion would be "kept by some French family of good character wherein the boarders shall be permitted to speak French only." In 1985 the large Victorian residence once home of the medical professor and faculty chairman Paul B. Barringer became La Maison Française. Soon thereafter, three other language houses were established—Max Kade (German), Casa Bolivar (Spanish), and the Russian House. In each, students became more fluent in another language and more familiar with another culture as part of their everyday lives. Native holidays were celebrated, foreign films viewed. Often the residence advisors of foreign language houses were themselves native speakers of those languages.

In other ways the university devoted its attention to undergraduates and their learning experience. The College of Arts and Sciences developed undergraduate seminars, small classes taught by the most eminent faculty members on special topics of interest, so undergraduates were assured the chance of contact with the great professors of the university. The Teaching Resource Center opened in 1990 to provide pedagogical support for graduate students, but it soon found that established professors wanted to use its services, too, participating in teaching workshops and requesting classroom critiques.

The Lively Arts

Since 1924 troupes of student actors—and members of the community, because female players were needed—had staged dramatic performances. For years the Virginia Players performed in a law school lecture room in Minor Hall modified into theater space. In 1974 the drama department moved into a building of its own. "We could fit all our Minor Hall facilities into our new scene shop alone," recalled LaVahn Hoh, a drama professor known for his one-of-a-kind course in circus history. The new drama building included Culbreth Theater, a large proscenium auditorium, and a smaller, adaptable "black box" theater, named after alumnus James Strother Helms, who was active in university drama until his death in 1959.

From this base, drama continued to enhance university life. Nationally distinguished cast members joined with Charlottesville locals every summer in performances by the Heritage Repertory Theater, founded in 1974. In 1989 Lewis M. Allen Jr., a theatrical producer and alumnus, chose the Culbreth Theater to preview his Broadway show *A Few Good Men*. Robert Chapel became chair of drama in 1990, bringing Broadway and Hollywood experience to the university. The film arts became more prominent from 1988 on, when the town began hosting an annual film festival. Established by the state's film office, the festival was adopted by the university in 1990. Four days of film screenings, panel discussions, and gala events brought

Living and learning together.
As the university grew, the ideal remained a community of learning, with teachers and students in close communication. Here Kenneth Elzinga (top), professor of economics, leads class discussion; Paul Gaston, professor of history, discusses a term paper with one of his students.

A diverse musical heritage.
From a string ensemble of 1900 to a jazz class of the 1990s, music has graced student life at the University of Virginia.

actors, directors, producers, and critics every October to the Virginia Film Festival.

In 1995 a newly restored Cabell Hall reopened, home for more musicians and composers than ever before. Just as, twenty years before, the Rotunda that it faces was restored through research to its original appearance, so Cabell Hall received similar care and treatment. Foyer walls returned to the burnt ochre color chosen by Stanford White in 1898, with pilasters painted a contrasting shade of terra cotta. The auditorium, too, returned to White's chosen tones, cream-colored walls trimmed with vibrant blue. New acoustical panels, refurbished seats, air-conditioning, and stage lighting were installed to satisfy modern demands unforeseen by White's contemporaries.

Faculty and students of the 1990s turned their attention to new musical forms like jazz and synthesizer composition. The musicologist Scott DeVeaux taught a course on the history of jazz, hosting performers in the classroom who enlivened his lectures. Judith Shatin, a composer whose works were performed at such university events as the inauguration of Robert O'Neil and Founder's Day 1993, spearheaded the development of a program in computer-based music. Students composed at computer workstations, creating music through digital synthesis as well as compositions for voice and instruments.

A Tradition of Great Writing

In the years after 1980, when the English department first granted the degree of master of fine arts, Virginia's creative writing program grew to national prominence, using a sizeable bequest to support aspiring poets and fiction writers. Teaching from 1967 until 1987, the fiction writer Peter Taylor greatly influenced the program. Sydney Blair, a novelist and creative writing instructor who studied with him, recalls that often Taylor would spend long periods of time in the classroom simply reading short stories aloud. "He had such a melodious voice," she says. "We were just supposed to listen. You would learn a lot about how to read a story as well as how to write one." At the age of seventy, in 1987, Taylor received the Pulitzer Prize for his novel *A Summons to Memphis.* His devotion to his art, despite a lack of critical attention before the Pulitzer Prize, says Blair, taught her the value of "writing what you must write, no matter what, and being undeterred by its reception."

Ann Beattie, Mary Lee Settle, Mark Strand, Paul Theroux, and Deborah Eisenberg all taught in the university's creative writing program at one time or another. Permanent faculty included John Casey, winner of the National Book Award for his novel *Spartina;* the poet Charles Wright, honored with a Pulitzer Prize for his poetry collection *Black Zodiac;* and Rita Dove,

Authors and professors. *From 1967 until his retirement in 1987, Peter Taylor (above) inspired young fiction writers. Young poets learned from Charles Wright and Rita Dove (left), both Pulitzer Prize winners. On 8 November 1994, Dove donated the university library's four millionth volume, "Lady Freedom among Us" (lower left), in both a bound and an electronic version.*

233

A new kind of college bookstore. *Opening its new quarters in 1994, the university bookstore offered a full range of scholarly and popular titles, textbooks, office supplies, and U.Va. clothing and gifts. More than simply a store, it also hosted lectures, readings, and concerts and established an endowment to support student programming and financial needs.*

another Pulitzer Prize–winning poet, who served as the U.S. poet laureate four years after joining the faculty. A special edition of Dove's poem "Lady Freedom among Us" was celebrated in November 1994 as the four millionth volume acquired by the university library. The poem was presented in two forms: as a book—a custom-designed, hand-printed art object—and in electronic form, accessible through the World Wide Web.

In 1998 the University Press of Virginia celebrated its thirty-fifth anniversary, its mission largely unchanged from that envisioned by President Edgar Shannon at its founding. "Creation at the University of Virginia of a scholarly press for the entire Virginia area," wrote the *Richmond Times-Dispatch* in 1963, "is a significant milestone in the state's intellectual advancement." The Press was, the editorial pointed out, unique in representing the entire academic community of the Commonwealth, not limiting itself to one university.

Since its inception the Press has published well over one thousand scholarly, regional, and general-interest books on a wide range of topics. Areas of particular strength have included southern studies, race studies, colonial history, Civil War history, Victorian literature and culture, gender studies, and religious studies. The Press has also published in partnership with other leading institutions throughout the state and beyond, including Colonial Williamsburg, the Virginia Historical Society, the Thomas Jefferson Memorial Foundation, and the National Portrait Gallery.

The university had operated an on-grounds bookstore in Newcomb Hall for almost forty years when, in October 1994, it opened a new bookstore, two stories tall, built atop a three-tier parking garage. A bookstore branch of Cavalier Computers opened soon thereafter as well as two satellite stores: Courts and Commerce, serving the graduate business and law schools, and T.J.'s Locker, a campus and sports shop located in the Aquatics and Fitness Center.

Working with departments throughout the university, including the creative writing program, the Women's Center, and the Office of African American Affairs, the bookstore staff hosted author lectures, readings by students, book fairs, and other literary and social events. Bookstore management and staff sought to interweave community and university service into their job of selling books. Theirs was among the first college bookstores to organize "Share Our Strength," a series of readings by distinguished local authors to raise funds to fight hunger and homelessness. By the late 1990s, the bookstore's success permitted it to support student programming financially and to contribute annually to an Endowment for Excellence, used in part to fund need-based scholarships. "We at the bookstore enjoy being a part of the university's academic mission and enriching our students' lives," says Jonathan Kates, bookstore director.

Rediscovering the Past

In 1993, excavating to expand a parking lot near Cabell Hall, a bulldozer struck something solid. University archaeologists determined that the blade had uncovered a coffin, one of twelve buried in the corner of a homesite long since forgotten. Faculty, students, and community members drew with curiosity to the site and helped unearth artifacts at the homesite of Catherine Foster, a free black woman who from the 1830s on ran her own business as a seamstress in a neighborhood just southeast of the Lawn. During the summer of 1994, graduate students turned fieldwork at the Foster site into a community experience. They talked with passers-by about their work and, once a week, instructed visitors on how to sift for artifacts that might reveal new insights into university history.

Shards of the past. *These artifacts emerged during the excavation of the house site of Catherine Foster, who owned property near the university in the 1830s.*

Turning with the same awareness to the Lawn itself, students and faculty have paid more attention in recent years to the legacy of African Americans from the university's early years. When Ishmail Conway, a professor of drama and director of the Luther P. Jackson Cultural Center, hosted black student visitors on a tour of university grounds, he encouraged them to look for the distinguishing marks that a slave of 1819 would have put on bricks he made. Conway also helped students stage historical interpretations of African Americans who played parts in the university's past, from Catherine Foster to the pioneering black students of the 1950s. Phyllis Leffler, director of the Institute for Public History, taught an undergraduate course on the history of the university and encouraged student projects that brought forgotten aspects to light. For example, one student, Alison

Learning from history. *Civil rights figure Julian Bond combines personal memories with historic research in his teaching.*

Laboratory sciences expand.
New buildings to house growing programs in the laboratory sciences were built along McCormick Road during the 1980s and 1990s. The engineering school built new quarters for its departments of materials science and chemical engineering, and the College of Arts and Sciences added wings to the chemistry and physics buildings and to Gilmer Hall (below) for the life sciences.

Linney, combed historic records for information on the slaves who built the Lawn and served students in the 1840s. As a university guide she incorporated her findings into tours of the Lawn.

Julian Bond, who joined the university faculty in 1993, helped students reconsider more recent African American history. One of the founders of the Student Nonviolent Coordinating Committee in the 1960s, Bond in 1998 became chairman of the national board of directors of the NAACP. Interspersing classroom discussions with memories of the days when he studied under Martin Luther King Jr. at Morehouse College, Bond represented for students an example of one who has lived the history he teaches.

A Dedication to Service

Since the latter part of the 1800s, the YMCA had organized students in missionary activities, operating out of offices in Madison Hall. By the late 1960s, however, student interest in Christian mission work had dwindled, and YMCA directors considered dissolving the chapter. A few undergraduates, led by the law student Samuel Manly, founded the Masters and Fellows of Madison Hall, a private non-profit corporation, run by a board of students, faculty, staff, and members of the Charlottesville community dedicated to social service. In 1975 the Masters and Fellows moved into their own house on Rugby Road. The organization was renamed Madison House, becoming in the 1980s one of the nation's largest collegiate volunteer programs dedicated to weekly community service activities. Through the 1990s three thousand students every year participated in day care, elderly care, hospital aide, Big Brother and Big Sister, and other community service programs. In 1992, Madison House initiated an "alternative spring break," helping students find humanitarian projects to which they could devote an entire vacation week.

Dedication to community service inspired a number of other organizations at the university through the 1990s. Led by the example of service fraternities, particularly those with traditionally African American memberships, fraternities, sororities, and the interfraternity and intersorority councils found ways for their members to contribute. Chi Omega sorority, for example, fostered literacy by reading to day-care and elementary school children and distributing bookmarks on grounds to heighten awareness of illiteracy. Members from four other sororities assisted in Special Olympics soccer games each week. Students formed dozens of other organizations, from a chapter of Amnesty International to a volunteer income-tax-assistance society, to offer service and answer needs in the larger community beyond the university grounds.

Madison House evolves. *Community service, administered through Madison Hall, has been an integral part of student life at the university for decades, from Bible-study classes in the 1940s to Santa visits in the 1990s. "I can honestly say I would not have stayed that first year without Madison House," says Elaine V. Cecelski, who after graduate study in sociology, went on to a career in community service, assisting the children of migrant workers in the Albemarle County school system.*

Into the Next Century

The University of Virginia was formed on a plan at once "broad and liberal and modern," in Jefferson's words. Those ideals still inspire university students, faculty, staff, and alumni, who seek to broaden the university's reach across the arts, sciences, and letters; who strive for an open forum of expression and debate; who discover and articulate new ideas through intellectual discourse, library research, and laboratory experimentation.

Some of the ideas that Jefferson brought into being at his university have become commonplace in American higher education: organization into disciplinary schools or departments; the elective system, whereby students choose their own courses of study; administration by democracy, through which faculty bear responsibility for curriculum and requirements. Other Jeffersonian ideas continue to distinguish the university: a nonsectarian atmosphere of inquiry and a student honor system. By the end of the twentieth century, the University of Virginia had fulfilled Jefferson's vision, educating future citizen-leaders not only from Virginia and the South but from the nation, the hemisphere, and the world.

Over many years people remarked that it felt as if Thomas Jefferson still lived at the University of Virginia—as though he were in the next room, just around the corner, still exerting an influence. His ideas continued to challenge. The principles of freedom, democracy, tolerance, and hope that he articulated in the eighteenth century and manifested in a nineteenth-century institution of learning remained driving ideals as the university entered the twenty-first century.

"The great object of our aim from the beginning," Jefferson wrote, "has been to make the establishment the most eminent in the United States." When *U.S. News and World Report* named the University of Virginia the best public university in the nation for the fifth year in a row, in 1998, some may have been tempted to consider Jefferson's goal met. But if he had been in the next room, just around the corner, he would have said that there was still work to be done. "Each generation," as he wrote in the Rockfish Gap Commission report of 1818, "must advance the knowledge and well-being of mankind, not *infinitely,* as some have said, but *indefinitely,* and to a term which no one can fix and forsee."

Notes

Chapter 1. The Vision

3 "Education . . . engrafts": "Report of the Commissioners," in Honeywell, 252.

4 "tending rapidly to ruin": Kale, *Hark,* 43.

5 "the indigence," "free children," "by this means": "A Bill for the More General Diffusion," in Honeywell, 204.

5 "We wish to establish": quoted in Kett, 241.

6 "high, dry, open": quoted in Shawen, 199.

7 By the end of 1817: Malone, *Sage,* 265.

8 "Pray drop me a line": quoted in Malone, *Sage,* 269–70.

11 "wherein all the branches": Shawen, app. 1.

11 a three-thousand-acre estate: "Report of the Commissioners," in Honeywell, 259–60.

13 "the Franklin": Honeywell, 125–26.

13 "Premature ideas": quoted in Ellis, 286.

Chapter 2. The Founding

16 "While you have been": quoted in Malone, *Sage,* 411.

17 "a plain small house": quoted in Wilson, ed., *Jefferson's Academical Village,* 11.

18 "that if the state should establish": Wilson, ed., *Jefferson's Academical Village,* 21.

18 "models of taste": Nichols, *Jefferson's Architectural Drawings,* 9.

20 "How charmingly": Wilson, ed., *Jefferson's Academical Village,* 54.

21 "Had we built a barn": Wilson, ed., *Jefferson's Academical Village,* 43.

23 "Our university is now so far advanced": Wilson, ed., *Jefferson's Academical Village,* 39.

24 "painted sky-blue": Bruce vol. 1, 270.

27 "preferring foreigners": quoted in Honeywell, 94.

27 "we shall never become": quoted in Honeywell, 131.

28 "acquiring esteem as fast": Malone, *Sage,* 410.

28 "an unreconstructed rebel": Clemons, *Notes on the Professors.*

29 While the cannons boomed: Culbreth, 142–44.

29 "rather a rough-looking German": quoted in Davis, *Correspondence,* 22.

29 "the violence said to have been": Minutes of the Board of Visitors, 14 September 1840.

31 "At his last visit": quoted in Patton and Doswell, 26.

Chapter 3. A University in Its Youth

39 two-hour block: "Regulations adopted by the Board . . . October 4, 1824," in Honeywell, 270.

40 "field evolutions": "Regulations adopted by the Board . . . October 4, 1824," in Honeywell, 275.

41 "If he be also": Minutes of the Board of Visitors, 16 July 1829.

44 One such student: Wall, 135–37.

45 "became dissolute": quoted in Quinn, 110.

50 "Masked students": Patton, *Jefferson, Cabell,* 67.

52 "The insubordination of our youth": quoted in Honeywell, 135.

52 "Professor Davis in the vigor": University Intelligence, *The Collegian* 3:2/3 (November/December 1840), 101.

52 "a nobler tradition": Thornton, "Honour System."

Honor

55 "internal force," "presuming": "College Law and Order," 314–15.

Chapter 4. War, Reconstruction, and Fire

61 "the pride of Virginia," "the recognized head": Collegiana, *Virginia University Magazine* 4:1 (October 1859), 42.

62 "noble statuary": Editors' Table, *Virginia University Magazine* 3:5 (February 1859), 269.

63 "splendid": O'Neal, *Pictorial History,* 54.

63 "*Ladies* especially": Collegiana, *Virginia University Magazine* 3:2 (November 1858), 88.

64 "said it would be the cause": Patton, *Jefferson, Cabell,* 189.

65 "a most useful": Collegiana, *Virginia University Magazine* 3:3 (December 1858), 150.

65 Typhoid fever swept through: Minutes of the Board of Visitors, 12 March, 19 March 1858.

65 "the Corner": Bruce vol. 5, 316–17.

66 "disguised atheism": Dashiell, 89.

66 "a most godless set": Dashiell, 91.

66 "succeeded beyond": Collegiana, *Virginia University Magazine* 3:6 (March 1859), 358.

66 number of "professors of religion": Collegiana, *Virginia University Magazine* 5:7 (April 1861), 380–81.

70 "The military spirit": "The Military Companies," *Virginia University Magazine* 5:5 (February 1861).

70 As the Southern Guard: Hutter.

70 "Then out to the lightning-rod": quoted in Patton, *Jefferson, Cabell,* 200–203.

70 "Things began to hum," "a hard but bloodless campaign": quoted in Patton, *Jefferson, Cabell,* 208–11.

71 "an awkward squad indeed": quoted in Patton, *Jefferson, Cabell,* 204–5.

71 "It didn't make no difference": "Uncle Henry: Bell-Ringer," *Corks and Curls* 1914, 150.

72 "with wandering thoughts": Minor, 48.

72 "the news *froze*": quoted in Brown, "Sheridan's Occupation," 39–40.

72 "We announced": Minor, 50.

72 "They were as civil": Minor, 55.

73 258 in 1865; 190 in 1866: University of Virginia Catalogue, 1866–67, 19.

73 regained enrollment more quickly: Moore, "The University and the Readjusters," 89.

73 One historian estimates: Moore, "The University and the Readjusters," 89.

74 "One cannot expect": University of Virginia Catalogue, 1890–91.

74 "didactic lectures": Davis, "History of the Medical Department."

74 "Think of a University": Editors' Table, *Virginia University Magazine* 4:6 (March 1860), 331.

76 "I have to be up": Bruce vol. 3, 330 n.

78 "Northern friend": Hantman, 66.

78 "cabinet of Natural Science": Hantman, 65.

78 "Here is a full procession": Hantman, 69.

79 "Mikado Tea": Dashiell, 101–10.

81 a personalized "hand-book": University of Virginia Catalogue, 1888–89.

81 "It sprang spontaneously": quoted in *Crust,* September 1946, 48.

81 "baths of every variety": Thornton, "Physical Culture," 23–27.

86 ladies below: Barringer, "Pleasant It Is," 27–29.

86 estimated to weigh: Vaughan and Gianniny, 143.

87 "It was an awful scene": Robinson, 17.

89 seventeen thousand were saved: Clemons to Wranek, 23 March 1955.

The Greeks

92 "At times sorority membership": Perry.

93 "It's meant to be impossible": Dickerson.

Chapter 5. Celebrating a Century

97 faculty conveyed: "The University Ablaze," 71–74.

98 "I'm scared to death": quoted in Wilson, "The Conflagration," 23.

99 "Until the fire, few people": quoted in Vaughan and Gianniny, xv.

101 "with nothing to do but lead": *University of Virginia,* 16.

101 "As a student I used to see": Friddell, 105.

103 Others saw it: Malone, *Alderman,* 195.

103 "the admission to this new department": Wagoner and Quantz, 4.

104 By 1902 a six-week institute: Wagoner and Quantz, 7.

104 "would be astonished": Whitney, 42.

104 Membership "denoted class": Bruce vol. 5, 277–78.

106 "When eight years old": Barringer, "Pleasant It Is," 8.

108 The 1906 event: *College Topics,* 18 April 1906.

108 not "as ugly": Collegiana, *Virginia University Magazine* 7:5/6 (February/March 1869), 285.

108 "Certainly in my day": Southall, 64.

108 "'Calico' was one pastime": Williams, *"Gay Nineties,"* 18.

111 In March 1917: Patton, "The University in the World War."

112 alumni in Europe wired Alderman: President's Papers, 1915–19, folder: "Founder's Day."

114 "If we had no other means": Bruce vol. 5, 424.

Athletics

116 "instructed the players forthwith": quoted in Bruce vol. 4, 144.

Chapter 6. Through Hard Times

123 "Like everyone else": Green, 133–34.

124 "the feminine touch": "Queen of Madison Hall."

124 "friendship and something like other-mothership":"Queen of Madison Hall."

126 "an almost passionate desire": Freeman.

127 "I knew that no one": Glendy, Dr. Margaret M., correspondence in Woody Material on Admission of Women.

127 "Her powers of acquisition": letter from Dean of Law to President Alderman, 1 January 1924, President's Papers.

131 He could multiply: Vaughan, *Rotunda Tales,* 11.

133 "He was the undisputed": Vaughan, *Rotunda Tales,* 162.

134 Alderman had identified: Rosenberg, 14–15.

134 "the beating heart": Clemons, "Proposed Specifications."

137 "the law school enrolled": Wagoner and Baxter, "Higher Education Goes to War," 411.

139 "While other students": Adams, "Stettinius Named."

140 more than 3,300 veterans: "University Is Receiving."

The Corner

142 In 1860 the women: Editors' Table, *Virginia University Magazine* 4:3 (December 1860), 159.

142 "plans for beautifying": "New Buildings Will Occupy Site of P.O.," *College Topics,* 29 January 1913.

142 "The university is attempting": "The Passing of the Corner," *College Topics,* 29 January 1913.

143 At the east end of the block: Eddins.

145 asked local merchants why: Hufford.

Chapter 7. The Capstone of Virginia Education

149 "Those who live": President's Annual Report, 1949.

150 "There has always been that 'ain't tellin'' look:" "Miss Mary B. Proffitt."

150 Colgate Darden considered her: Bice.

151 it was to be a "hangout": Newman.

152 to "refuse respectfully": Statement by the Board of Visitors, 29 September 1935, in President's Papers.

152 Jackson accepted $75: Williams, "Though Rejected."

153 refused an offer: Minutes of the Faculty, 25 April 1951.

153 "This marks the first time": Jordan.

157 Some say: personal interviews with Shea, Whitehead, Gianniny.

157 groundbreaking work in physics: Fowle; Beams.

161 "I wrote James Southall Wilson": Becker.

The Professional Schools

164 A janitor: Davis, "Old Times," 115.

164 One medical alumnus remembered: Morton, 23.

165 "The hospital would be called": quoted in Matthews, 79.

165 "a model for the nation": quoted in President's Report, 1988–89.

166 "cut the law into thin slices": quoted in Ritchie, 29.

166 "a precise counterpart": quoted in Ritchie, 35.

166 "We find ourselves": quoted in Ritchie, 64.

167 "the only fowl": quoted in Ritchie, 89.

167 "It is in the South": "The Virginia Law School."

168 "No exclusively graduate": in preface to Sheppard, 10.

169 "You don't even know": quoted in Shenkir and Wilkerson, 104.

Chapter 8. A Time of Change

173 with sponsored research revenues up: President's Report, 1971–72.

174 "to honor the honorable": From the Editors, *Plume and Sword,* 13 October 1961.

175 "guaranteed to blow your mind": "Slithy Toves."

177 "near death": Shea, "University Protest Rekindled."

177 "I and some others said": Clement, oral history interview.

178 Whit Clement remembered: Clement, oral history interview.

179 "did more than anything": Roebuck, oral history interview.

179 "As we meet here": Shannon.

180 "a rallying point": "The President Speaks."

180 "Shannon looks very much": "The University Bows."

180 "there are times": Fuller, "Shannon Defends Rights."

180 "I live it": Crystal, 2.

181 "And nobody ever wore socks": Gunter.

184 Virginia Anne Scott went to work: Phalen, 33–36.

191 Knowing that Hirsch: Guernsey.

191 "best-designed functional building": "Biology Head Lauds Interior."

193 "a first-rate academic institution": McNett.

Beyond the Lawn

196 "the most significant building": "Architecture."

Chapter 9. Restoring Ideals

201 "Once again": Nichols, "Phoenix," 27.

202 "We had no information": quoted in Vaughan and Gianniny, 107.

204 "a trip to the source": quoted in President's Report, 1975–76.

209 "Too bad": Culpepper.

209 "We are a terrible": Silverman.

210 "Easters was not": Woody, oral history interview.

210 "For the uninitiate": Vanguardia, *Virginia Spectator,* April 1938, 4.

Chapter 10. A University of the Twenty-first Century

229 "The Public Ivy is withering": Leslie, 64–65.

231 "We could fit": "Stage Presence."

237 "I could honestly say": Cecelski.

Works Cited

Quotations in the present tense (for example, " . . . says John T. Casteen") derive from the following personal and telephone interviews conducted during the research for this book: Berkeley, Frank L., Jr., 2 June 1998. Bice, Raymond C., 18 June, 29 June 1998. Blackford, Staige D., 4 June 1998. Blair, Sydney, by telephone, 23 September 1998. Brandt, Richard, 16 June 1998. Britton, Rick, 24 July 1998. Brodie, Barbara, 7 April 1998. Canevari, Robert, 9 June 1998. Casteen, John T., III, 12 June 1998. Cherry, Kelly, by telephone, 20 July 1998. Conway, Ishmail, 20 July 1998. Crotty, Eugene, by telephone, 5 June 1998. Day, Douglas, 21 July 1998. Dillard, Richard, by telephone, 17 July 1998. Dolan, Robert, e-mail correspondence, 24 September 1998. Fishback, William H., 20 May 1998. Forbes, John, 4 June 1998. Garrett, George, 3 July 1998. German, Sandra, 19 June 1998. Gianniny, O. Allan, Jr., 10 June 1998. Gilliam, Alexander G., 23 June 1998. Gunter, Bradley, 29 June 1998. Handy, Alice W., 8 June 1998. Hereford, Frank L., Jr., 6 May 1998. Hirsch, E. D., Jr., 14 January 1999, by telephone. Howard, F. Murray, 15 June, 7 July, 15 July 1998. Hunt, C. Ray, 21 July 1998. Johnson, Floyd E., 22 July 1998. Lay, C. Edward, 8 September 1998. Mincer, Robert, 5 August 1998. Mitchell, Edward, 5 June 1998. Moran, Charles L., Jr., 1 June 1998. O'Neil, Robert M., 29 May 1998. Parr, Mary Ann, 13 August 1998. Rinehart, Jill, 27 May 1998. Seward, George, by telephone, 25 September 1998. Shea, Vincent, 11 June 1998. Sullivan, Gilbert, 2 April 1998. Taylor, Henry, by telephone, 17 July 1998. Terry, Sylvia, 17 July 1998. Turner, M. Rick, 8 July 1998. Vaughan, Joseph L., 19 May 1998. Wagoner, Jennings, 3 July 1998. Whitehead, W. Dexter, 23 April 1998.

A number of University of Virginia documents and publications have also proven valuable in the research for this book, namely: Minutes of the Faculty; Minutes of the Board of Visitors; Presidents' Annual Reports; University of Virginia Catalogue; *Corks and Curls* (student yearbook); *College Topics* and the *Cavalier Daily* (student newspapers); student magazines from over the years, including the *Collegian*, the *Virginia University Magazine*, the *Virginia Spectator*, the *Virginia Reel, Crust, Plume and Sword*, and *Rapier; Inside UVa* (an internal newspaper); and alumni publications, including *Alumni Bulletin* and *Alumni News* and others originating in various schools and departments.

Adams, Doug. "Stettinius Named Secretary of State," *College Topics,* 1 December 1944.

"Architecture." *Alumni News* 58, no. 4 (March–April 1970).

Barringer, Anna. "Pleasant It Is to Remember These Things." *Magazine of Albemarle County History* 24 (1965–1966).

Beams, J. W. "High-Speed Rotation." *Physics Today* 12, no. 7 (July 1959).

Becker, Robert. "Rare Book Donation 'Priceless.'" *Charlottesville Daily Progress,* 22 June 1986.

"Biology Head Lauds Gilmer Hall Interior." *Cavalier Daily,* 5 November 1963.

Bruce, Philips Alexander. *History of the University of Virginia, 1819–1919.* 5 vols. New York: Macmillan, 1920–22.

Cecelski, Elaine V. Letter in Madison House scrapbook.

Clement, Whittington W. Oral history interview, 25 March 1977. University Archives. RG-26/228.

Clemons, Harry. Letter to William Wranek, 23 March 1955. University Archives. File "General Records, Alderman Library, 1955–1959." RG-4/2/6.631.

—. *Notes on the Professors for Whom the University of Virginia Halls and Residence Houses are Named.* Charlottesville: University of Virginia Press, 1961.

—. "Proposed Specifications for a New Library Building at the University of Virginia." 16 June 1933. University Archives. President's Papers, 1930–1933. Folder "Library (1)." RG-2/1/2.491.

"College Law and Order." *Virginia University Magazine* 4, no. 6 (March 1860).

Crystal, Charlotte. "Sabato: Talking to the Media Is Talking to the Public." *Inside UVa,* 10 October 1997, 2.

Dabney, Virginius. *Far Echoes from the Old Arcades: A History of the Alumni Association of the University of Virginia.* Charlottesville: Alumni Association of the University of Virginia, 1983.

Dashiell, David W. "'Between Earthly Wisdom and Heavenly Truth': The Effort to Build a Chapel at the University of Virginia, 1835–1890." *Magazine of Albemarle County History* 52 (1994).

Davis, D. C. T. "Old Times at the University." *Alumni Bulletin* 4, no. 4 (February 1898).

Davis, John Staige. "History of the Medical Department of the University of Virginia 1825–1914." *Alumni Bulletin* (July 1914).

Davis, Richard Beale, ed. *Correspondence of Thomas Jefferson and Francis Walker Gilmer, 1814–1826.* Columbia: University of South Carolina Press, 1946.

Dickerson, Jeffrey. "Black Frats: Personal Advancement through Service Is a Way of Life for These UVa Students." *Charlottesville Daily Progress,* 15 May 1977.

"Dinamo Taxed." *College Topics,* 18 April 1906.

Dunnington, Bell. To Sadie [Dunnington]. 28 October 1895. University Archives. University News Office. File "Rotunda."

Eddins, Joe. *Around the Corner after World War I.* Charlottesville: Joseph C. Eddins, 1977.

Ellis, Joseph J. *American Sphinx: The Character of Thomas Jefferson.* New York: Alfred A. Knopf, 1997.

Flannagan, Roy. E-mail posting to Shakespeare Electronic Conference, 2, no. 126, 4 May 1991.

Fowle, Farnsworth. "Jesse W. Beams, 78; Top Physicist, Dies." *New York Times,* 25 July 1977.

Freeman, Anne Hobson. "Mary Munford's Fight for a College for Women Co-ordinate with the University of Virginia." *Virginia Magazine of History and Biography* 78, no. 4 (October 1970).

Friddell, Guy. *Colgate Darden: Conversations with Guy Friddell.* Charlottesville: University Press of Virginia, 1978.

Fuller, Ralph. "Shannon Defends Rights of Dissent, Free Expression." *Richmond Times-Dispatch,* 8 June 1970, 1.

Goode, James Moore. "'Old Guff' in Virginia." *Virginia Cavalcade* 16, no. 1 (Summer 1966).

Green, Julian. *Love in America: 1919–1922.* Vol. 3 of *Autobiography.* Trans. Euan Cameron. New York and London: Marion Boyars, 1994.

Guernsey, Lisa. "The House That Bowers Built." *Alumni News* (Spring 1995): 27.

Handbook for Women Students. University Archives. Dean of Women's Archival Files. RG-23/3, no. 9237-B.

Hantman, Jeffrey L. "Brooks Hall at the University of Virginia: Unravelling the Mystery." *Magazine of Albemarle County History* 47 (1989).

Honeywell, Roy J. *The Educational Work of Thomas Jefferson.* Cambridge, Mass.: Harvard University Press, 1931.

Hufford, Mark. "Time Stops on the Corner, but Conversation Doesn't." *Cavalier Daily,* 28 April 1977.

Hutter, Edward S. "Sketch of the University at the Commencement of the War." *Corks and Curls,* 1890.

The Inauguration of Edgar Finley Shannon, Jr. as President of the University of Virginia. Charlottesville: University of Virginia, 1959.

Jordan, Ervin L., Jr. "Walter N. Ridley: U.Va.'s First Black Graduate." *Charlottesville-Albemarle Tribune,* 3 October 1996.

Kale, Wilford. *Hark upon the Gale: An Illustrated History of the College of William and Mary.* Norfolk, Va.: Donning Co., 1985.

—. "'Public Ivys' Lists U.Va., W&M among Top State-Supported Schools." *Richmond Times-Dispatch,* 19 August 1985.

Kett, Joseph F. "Education." In *Thomas Jefferson: A Reference Biography,* ed. Merrill D. Peterson. New York: Charles Scribner's Sons, 1986.

Leslie, Frank. "The Lewis Brooks Museum of Natural Science." *Illustrated Magazine,* 1878.

Malone, Dumas. *Edwin A. Alderman: A Biography.* New York: Doubleday, Doran & Co. 1940.

—. *The Sage of Monticello: Jefferson and His Time.* Vol. 6. Boston: Little, Brown and Co., 1981.

Marshall, Hunter Holmes. Letter to William Cabell Carrington, 19 November 1840. University of Virginia Special Collections. Papers of H. H. Marshall. Accession #7069.

Matthews, Sarah S. *The University of Virginia Hospital: Its First Fifty Years.* Charlottesville: Michie Co., 1960.

McNett, Ian. "UVa Enters the Twentieth Century." *Change* (Winter 1972–73).

Minor, John B. "John B. Minor's Civil War Diary." Edited by Anne Freudenberg and John Casteen. *Magazine of Albemarle County History* 22 (1963–4): 45–55.

"Miss Mary B. Proffit." *Alumni News* (October 1944): 8.

Moore, James T. "The University and the Readjusters." *Virginia Magazine of History and Biography* 78, no. 1 (January 1970).

Morton, C. Bruce, II. *History of the Department of Surgery, School of Medicine, University of Virginia, Charlottesville, Virginia, 1824–1971.* Charlottesville: Division of Medical Art and Photography, University of Virginia Medical Center, [1971].

Nelson, Charles E., ed. *Stringfellow Barr: A Centennial Appreciation of His Life and Work.* Annapolis, Md.: St. John's College Press, 1997.

"New Buildings Will Occupy Site of P.O." *College Topics,* 29 January 1913.

Newman, J. Notes, 8 August 1947. University Archives. President's Papers. Box 11, folder "Annual Reports." RG-2/1/2.55-II.

Nichols, Frederick D. "Phoenix in Virginia." *Arts in Virginia* 1, no. 3 (Spring 1961).

—. *Thomas Jefferson's Architectural Drawings.* Charlottesville: Thomas Jefferson Memorial Foundation and the University Press of Virginia, 1978.

"The Passing of the Corner." *College Topics,* 29 January 1913.

Patton, John S. *Jefferson, Cabell and the University of Virginia.* New York and Washington, D.C.: Neale Publishing Co., 1906.

—. "The University of Virginia in the World War." University of Virginia Library, Microfilm 7058.3. Charlottesville: University of Virginia, 1927.

Patton, John S., and Sallie J. Doswell. *The University of Virginia: Glimpses of Its Past and Present.* Lynchburg, Va.: J.P. Bell Co., Printers, 1900.

Perry, Alice. "U.Va. Sororities Number Three." *Charlottesville Daily Progress,* 24 March 1960.

Phalen, Kathleen F. "John Lowe: Lightning Rod for Civil Liberties." *UVA Lawyer* (Winter 1996): 31–38.

"The President Speaks." *Cavalier Daily,* 11 May 1970, 2.

"Queen of Madison Hall." *Alumni News* (November 1943): 6.

Quinn, Arthur Hobson. *Edgar Allan Poe: A Critical Biography.* New York: Appleton-Century-Crofts, Inc., 1941.

"Report of Committee on Machinery of Honor System." *College Topics,* 15 May 1909.

Ritchie, John. *The First Hundred Years: A Short History of the School of Law of the University of Virginia for the Period 1826–1926.* Charlottesville: University Press of Virginia for the University of Virginia School of Law, 1978.

Robinson, Morgan Poitiaux. *The Burning of the Rotunda.* Richmond, Va.: F. J. Mitchell Printing Co., [1921].

Roebuck, James. Oral history interview, 12 January 1994. University Archives. RG-26/209.

Rosenberg, Chester. "President Alderman and the New Library." *Virginia Spectator,* May 1938.

Shannon, Edgar F., Jr. Typescript, 10 May 1970. University Archives. President's Papers. Box 57, folder "Speeches." RG-2/1/2.741.

Shawen, Neil McDowell. *The Casting of a Lengthened Shadow: Thomas Jefferson's Role in Determining the Site for a State University in Virginia.* Ed.D. dissertation. Washington, D.C.: George Washington University, 1980.

Shea, Peter. "University Protest Rekindled after Near Death Yesterday." *Cavalier Daily,* 8 May 1970.

Shenkir, William G., and William R. Wilkerson. *University of Virginia's McIntire School of Commerce: The First Seventy-Five Years, 1921–1996.* Charlottesville: McIntire School of Commerce, 1996.

Sheppard, C. Stewart, ed. *The First Twenty Years: The Darden School at Virginia.* Charlottesville: Darden Graduate Business School Sponsors of the University of Virginia, 1975.

Siepel, Kevin H. *Rebel: The Life and Times of John Singleton Mosby.* New York: St. Martin's Press, 1983.

Silverman, Joel. "Welsh: 'We Are a Terrible Football Team.'" *Cavalier Daily,* 11 October 1982.

Simms, L. Moody, Jr. "Philip Francis du Pont and the University of Virginia." *Magazine of Albemarle County History* 31 (1973).

"Slithy Toves to Entertain." *Cavalier Daily,* 15 May 1968.

Southall, James P. C. *In the Days of My Youth: When I Was a Student in the University of Virginia, 1888–1893.* Chapel Hill: University of North Carolina Press, 1947.

"Stage Presence." *Of Arts and Sciences* 7, no. 2 (Spring 1990).

Thornton, William Mynn. "The Honour System at the University of Virginia in Origin and Use." *Sewanee Review* (January 1907).

—. "Physical Culture at the University of Virginia." *Alumni Bulletin* 1, no. 1 (July 1894).

Tucker, George. *The Life of Thomas Jefferson.* Vol. 2. Philadelphia: Carey, Lea & Blanchard, 1837.

Tutwiler, H. *Early Years of the University of Virginia.* Address before the Alumni Society of the University of Virginia, June 29, 1882. Charlottesville: Charlottesville Book and Job Office, 1882.

"The University Ablaze." *Alumni Bulletin* 2, no. 3 (November 1895).

"The University Bows." *Richmond Times-Dispatch,* 12 May 1970.

"University Cowed by High-Strung Angus Steer." *Cavalier Daily,* 6 May 1965.

University History Officer. *Brief Biographical Sketches of the Professors for Whom the Dormitories at the University of Virginia Were Named.* April 1978. University Archives. RG-30/5.781.

"University Is Receiving Over Million Dollars for Veteran's [*sic*] Schooling." *College Topics,* 24 October 1946.

The University of Virginia in the Life of the Nation: Academic Addresses Delivered on the Occasion of the Installation of Edward Anderson Alderman as President of the University of Virginia. Brooklyn, N.Y.: Eagle Press, 1905.

Vaughan, Joseph L. *Rotunda Tales: Stories from the University of Virginia, 1920–1960.* Charlottesville: University of Virginia Alumni Association, 1991.

Vaughan, Joseph L., and O. Allan Gianniny Jr. *Thomas Jefferson's Rotunda Restored, 1973–1976.* Charlottesville: University Press of Virginia, 1981.

"The Virginia Law School." *University of Virginia Magazine,* November 1960.

Wagoner, Jennings L., Jr., and Robert L. Baxter Jr. "Higher Education Goes to War: The University of Virginia's Response to World War II." *Virginia Magazine of History and Biography,* July 1992.

Wagoner, Jennings L, Jr., and Richard Quantz. "Public Education, the University of Virginia and the Curry School of Education: The Beginnings of a Tradition." Presented at the Society of Professors of Education, Denver, Colorado, 1985.

Wall, Charles Coleman, Jr. *Students and Student Life at the University of Virginia, 1825 to 1861.* Ph.D. dissertation. Charlottesville: University of Virginia, 1978.

Wertenbaker, Charles J. "Honor." *Saturday Evening Post,* 3 August 1929.

Whitney, Mary E. "Women and the University." Unpublished paper, February 1969. University Archives. Papers of T. Braxton Woody on the Admission of Women. File 1982-A, box 2.

Williams, Lewis C. *The "Gay Nineties" at the University of Virginia.* Charlottesville: Michie Co., 1942.

Wilson, Richard Guy. "The Conflagration and the Making of the 'New' University." In *"Arise and Build!" A Centennial Commemoration of the 1895 Rotunda Fire.* Charlottesville: University of Virginia Library Special Collections, 1995.

—, ed. *Thomas Jefferson's Academical Village.* Charlottesville: Bayly Museum of the University of Virginia, 1993.

Woody, T. Braxton. Material on the Admission of Women. University Archives. Accession 1982-A, B.

—. Oral history interview, 20 November 1975. University Archives. RG-26/45.

Further Reading

The first full history of the university, published at its centennial in 1921, was the five-volume *History of the University of Virginia* by Philip Alexander Bruce. Virginius Dabney's *Mr. Jefferson's University* begins where Bruce leaves off and focuses on twentieth-century history up to the Hereford administration and the 1970s. William B. O'Neal's *Pictorial History of the University of Virginia* (second edition published 1976) offers many images, with an architectural focus, from the founding to 1976. John Hammond Moore's *Albemarle: Jefferson's County, 1727–1976* helps place the university's history in the context of its larger community, as does *Charlottesville and the University of Virginia: A Pictorial History* by Fred T. Heblich and Mary Ann Elwood (1982), which includes many interesting images and information about town and gown into the 1980s.

On the Founding of the University
The sixth volume of *Jefferson and His Time*, Dumas Malone's biography of Jefferson, is entitled *The Sage of Monticello* (1981) and contains significant strands of information on Jefferson's work toward building the university. The ideas behind the founding of the university are analyzed in Roy J. Honeywell's *The Educational Work of Thomas Jefferson* (1931). Gene Crotty's *Jefferson's Legacy: His Own University* (1998) focuses on the Rockfish Gap Commission meeting and decisions to position the university in Charlottesville.

On the Architecture of the University
Published in conjunction with an exhibit at the Bayly Art Museum, *Thomas Jefferson's Academical Village: The Creation of an Architectural Masterpiece*, edited by Richard Guy Wilson (1995), incorporates interesting articles and a wealth of architectural images. Pendleton Hogan's *The Lawn: A Guide to Jefferson's University* (1987) is a handy visitors' guide. A longer study of university buildings and their history can be found in *University of Virginia: An Architectural Tour* by Richard Guy Wilson and Sara A. Butler (1999). Joseph L. Vaughan and O. Allan Gianniny Jr. detail the 1970s-era Rotunda restoration very well in *Thomas Jefferson's Rotunda Restored, 1973–1976* (1981).

On Student Life
Several memoirs and reminiscences focus on life at the University of Virginia. While some are dated in style and language, each gives an intensely personal glimpse of the university. David M. R. Culbreth, M.D., recalls students and professors of the 1870s in *The University of Virginia: Memories of Her Student-Life and Professors* (1908). John S. Patton and Sallie J. Doswell's *The University of Virginia: Glimpses of Its Past and Present* (1900) offers insight into student life at the turn of the century. Joseph L. Vaughan's *Rotunda Tales: Stories from the University of Virginia, 1920–1960* (1991) features anecdotes and personality profiles of presidents and professors of the middle of the twentieth century.

On the University during the Civil War
Ervin L. Jordan Jr.'s *Charlottesville and the University of Virginia in the Civil War* (1988) offers a detailed historic account of the war's effect on the university and surrounding communities.

On University of Virginia Presidents
Dumas Malone wrote the authoritative biography *Edwin A. Alderman, A Biography* (1940). Guy Friddell's 1978 volume *Colgate Darden: Conversations with Guy Friddell* includes a number of comments from Darden on his days as a student, then as president, of the university.

Illustration Credits

University of Virginia

Alumni Association: 45 (left), 57 (top), 75 (bottom), 91 (center), 99, 101, 103, 106, 116 (lower left), 123 (top), 136, 143 (top right), 145 (bottom), 149, 152 (bottom), 158 (left), 166 (left), 167 (right), 170–71, 173 (top), 176, 181, 182 (top), 193, 195 (top right), 196, 201 (top), 205 (bottom), 211 (inset), 213 (center), 229 (top).

Courtesy of University of Virginia Bookstore: 217 (center).

Darden School: 168, 169, 197 (photographer: Jack Mellott).

Office of the Dean of Students: 177 (bottom).

Facilities Management Resource Center: 198–99, 202 (top), 230 (bottom).

Law School Foundation: 127 (Ned Bittinger, painter and photographer), 166 (bottom), 167 (left).

Papers of Thomas Jefferson, Special Collections, Alderman Library: 6, 8, 11, 19 (bottom), 20, 24 (top), 25 (right), 50 (right), 202 (bottom).

Special Collections, Alderman Library: 1, 3 (bottom), 7 (top right), 9, 14–15, 17 (top), 20, 20–21, 26 (bottom), 27, 28 (foreground), 33, 36–37, 39, 40, 41, 43, 45 (right), 48, 49, 51 (bottom), 56, 57 (bottom), 58–59, 59, 61, 62, 63, 64, 65, 67, 70 (left), 71, 72–73, 73, 74, 75 (top), 76 (top), 76 (bottom), 78 (bottom), 79, 81 (bottom), 82, 83 (bottom), 85 (top), 86, 87, 88, 89, 90 (bottom), 91 (bottom), 94–95, 96, 97, 98, 100 (top left), 100–101, 103, 104, 105 (left), 106 (top and lower left), 107 (bottom), 108, 109, 110, 111 (bottom), 112 (top), 113, 114, 115, 116 (top center), 117 (right), 118 (lower left), 120–21, 121, 123 (bottom), 124 (top), 125 (bottom), 126, 129, 130, 131 (right), 133, 134, 135, 136, 137, 138, 139, 140, 141, 142 (bottom), 143 (top left, bottom), 143, 146–47, 147, 150, 151, 153, 156, 157 (bottom), 159, 160 (top), 161, 164, 171, 173 (bottom), 177 (top), 178, 185 (right), 194 (bottom right), 204 (inset), 232 (inset), 237 (top).

Stephanie Gross for University of Virginia Neurosciences: 229 (bottom).

Center for Nursing Historical Inquiry, School of Nursing: 125 (top).

Courtesy of University Relations: 180, 190, 205 (top), 221.

Other Sources

Jim Carpenter: 119 (left).

Tom Cogill: 32, 34 (bottom), 35, 131 (left), 172, 192, 212, 222 (left), 223 (left), 224, 233 (left), 235.

Lionel Delevingne: 221 (upper left), 222 (right).

Bill Denison: 214 (top), 231 (bottom).

Bill Faust: 218.

Courtesy of the Frances Loeb Library, Graduate School of Design, Harvard University: 194 (bottom left).

Todd Harry Friedlander: ix, 196–97.

Erin Garvey: 42, 44, 54 (right), 81 (top), 85 (bottom), 90 (top), 105 (right), 106 (right), 107 (top), 108–9, 112 (bottom), 116 (center), 174, 179, 207 (bottom), 208 (center), 233 (bottom).

Courtesy of O. Allan Gianniny Jr.: 204 (top), 220.

Gleason/Viscom: 4.

Susan Tolleson Gowen: 51 (top).

Daniel Grogan: 7 (bottom), 15 (inset), 18 (top), 22–23, 24 (bottom), 26 (top), 29 (top), 30–31, 50 (left), 60, 68–69, 77, 92–93, 111 (upper right), 117 (top), 118 (top), 132, 160 (bottom), 165, 182 (bottom), 186–87, 188, 189, 195 (center), 199, 200, 202 (center), 203, 205, 207 (top), 208 (bottom), 209, 214 (left), 215, 216, 223 (right), 225, 232 (top), 233 (center), 236.

Peggy Harrison: 206, 227 (top).

Frank C. Hartman, courtesy of the Albemarle County Historical Society: 152 (top).

Courtesy of Harry Henderson: 92, 183.

Courtesy of Elizabeth Meade Howard: 124 (left), 142 (top).

Courtesy of Kappa Delta Sorority: 93 (center).

Katherine Kayser: 227 (bottom).

Scott Keeney: 91 (top), 210.

Rob Krupicka: 70 (right).

Pete LaFleur: 119 (right).

Library of Congress: 18 (bottom).

The Library of Virginia: 21 (top).

Robert Llewellyn: 2, 53.

Madison House Archives: 237 (inset).

Monticello/Thomas Jefferson Memorial Foundation: 3 (top; gift of Mr. and Mrs. Carl W. Smith, Mr. and Mrs. T. Eugene Worrell), 5 (photographer: L. Phillips).

Philadelphia Museum of Art: 194 (center).

Ed Roseberry: 93 (right), 175, 184, 185 (left), 201 (bottom), 224–25.

Dave Sagarin: ii–iii.

Bill Sublette: vi, 1 (inset), 10, 12, 13, 16, 17 (bottom), 19 (top), 25 (left), 28 (background), 29 (bottom), 34 (top), 37, 38, 46–47, 54 (left), 55, 66, 78 (top), 80, 84, 95 (inset), 100 (center), 102, 122, 128, 144, 148, 154–55, 211 (top), 213 (top), 217 (top, bottom), 219, 228, 230 (top), 231 (top), 233 (right), 234, 239.

Ralph Thompson: 157 (top), 158 (right), 162, 163, 166, 208 (top).

Mei-Lei Tsou: 145 (top).

Valentine Museum, Richmond, Virginia: 83 (top).

Index